Teachers' Guide

Non-fiction writing

SCAFFOLDS

Written by
Dennis Watts

HOPSCOTCH
EDUCATIONAL PUBLISHING

Published by
Hopscotch Educational Publishing Ltd
Unit 2
The Old Brushworks
56 Pickwick Road
Corsham
Wiltshire
SN13 9BX

01249 701701

© 2003 Hopscotch Educational Publishing

Written by Dennis Watts
Series design by Blade Communications
Cover illustration by Kirsty Wilson
Illustrated by Jane Bottomley
Printed by Athenaeum Press Ltd, Gateshead

ISBN 1-904307-32-9

Dennis Watts hereby asserts his moral right to be
identified as the author of this work in accordance
with the Copyright, Designs and Patents Act, 1988.

Non-fiction writing
SCAFFOLDS

CONTENTS

Non-fiction writing scaffolds for Year 3

INTRODUCTION

Non-fiction Writing Scaffolds Year 3 is intended for use in schools to help teach children how to write effectively in a variety of non-fiction genres. It improves children's ability to organise their writing so that it has purpose by familiarising them with a system of planning which they can apply to any title. As they work through the units, the children assemble a portfolio of non-fiction texts containing genre-specific vocabulary and writing features. The chosen text types coincide with those in the Literacy Framework's text-level objectives.

Many non-fiction texts are essentially cross-curricular. Thus the ability to write specifically and purposefully about a subject will benefit other areas of study.

Each unit includes information and activities on at least one sentence-level objective. Therefore the book also enhances the children's knowledge of grammar, punctuation and style.

THE PROGRAMME CONTAINS:

a teachers' book comprising:

- notes for teachers on the genres
- a bibliography for each genre
- copies of exemplar texts together with teaching notes
- guidance on how to develop grammar and punctuation skills in children's writing
- guidance on how to write in the particular genre and on specific features of each non-fiction text.

a resource book of photocopiable material comprising:

- illustrated versions of the exemplar texts especially produced for children
- notes for the children on understanding the grammar and punctuation (optional reference material)
- photocopiable activity sheets to reinforce the grammar and punctuation (optional)
- notes and tips for the children on writing non-fiction texts (optional reference material)
- differentiated scaffolds which give the children choices and guide them through the course of the text they are about to write
- vocabulary banks for them to use and add to.

HOW TO USE THE PROGRAMME

1 After examining texts in the target genre, read and discuss the exemplar text with the children, using the notes in the margin to highlight the examples of the unit's teaching point and writing feature. The children should follow the text using their own illustrated version from the resource book.

2 Next, read through and explain the 'Understanding the grammar and punctuation' section of the unit. The children can do the activities together, either orally or using whiteboards, or independently on paper.

3 Then explain the 'Helpful hints' and 'Writing features' sections of the unit to the children.

4 Read through the scaffolds with the children. Then give them the differentiated word banks and ask them to record their own vocabulary suggestions in the space provided.

5 Give the children time to plan, write and edit their non-fiction text. Each child can then store the best copies in a writing folder.

NOTES

When using the scaffolds, give the children strict time limits to plan and write each of the sections. This will give them practice in writing timed non-fiction texts as preparation for the Key Stage 2 writing test.

However, the system is entirely flexible. The activities in each unit, from reading the exemplar to composing their own text using the scaffolds, can be used in shared or guided time, with the children working collaboratively or individually.

The order of activities for each unit corresponds exactly with the sequence for the teaching of writing outlined in Grammar for Writing (DfEE 0107/200). First the model can be discussed and its grammatical and thematic features interrogated during shared reading. Next the grammar and punctuation activities can be undertaken to reinforce the children's understanding of the relevant sentence-level objectives. The helpful hints section, scaffolds, and vocabulary banks support the teacher and children in shared writing sessions and in subsequent guided and independent writing.

The method works well with children of all abilities and with bilingual pupils, as it offers the security of a detailed framework and a bank of appropriate vocabulary together with the challenge of a grammar and writing features component for each unit.

The units fulfil the text-level and sentence-level requirements of the NLS Framework for Year 3 and revise components from Year 2. The units may be used specifically in literacy lessons or they may be linked with work in other curriculum areas and used accordingly.

TERM 1
UNIT 1

Genre: reports – information texts (T21; T22)
Grammar: verbs and verb tenses (S3; S4)
Punctuation: revision of capital letters and full stops (S11; S12)
Writing feature: organising and presenting ideas, labelled diagrams (T21; T22)

UNIT 2

Genre: reports – holiday guides (T22)
Grammar: verbs; verb tenses (S3; S4) use of third person
Punctuation: devices for presenting text (S9)
Writing features: headlines, presentation, content, language and layout (T21; T22)

UNIT 3

Genre: instructions – making or doing something
Grammar: verbs, especially second person verbs for instructional writing (S10) adjectives for clarity (not effect) (S2)
Punctuation: commas for lists (S6; S7)
Writing features: how instructions are organised – numbering, lists (T14; T16)

TERM 2
UNIT 4

Genre: instructions – directions
Grammar: plurals (S4)
Punctuation: use of capitalisation (S8)
Writing features: the importance of sequencing and diagrams (T16; T21)

UNIT 5

Genre: note taking – historical information
Grammar: deleting words and retaining meaning (S9)
Punctuation: commas (S6; S7)
Writing: how to make notes, identifying key words, using simple formats for notes, using shortened forms of words (T17; T20; T25; T26)

UNIT 6

Genre: recounts – informal letters
Grammar: pronouns (S2)
Punctuation: letter punctuation (S12; S8)
Writing features: features of personal letters, email messages, style and vocabulary appropriate to reader (T20)

TERM 3
UNIT 7

Genre: recounts – formal letters
Grammar: grammatical agreement of pronouns and verbs (S3)
Punctuation: organising letters into paragraphs (S23)
Writing features: features of formal letters selecting appropriate style and vocabulary (T20)

UNIT 8

Genre: recounts – newspaper reports
Grammar: adjectives to get attention and interest (S2), verbs – past tense (S4)
Punctuation: dialogue punctuation (S4)
Writing features: features of newspaper reports (T22, T21)

UNIT 9

Genre: explanations: encyclopaedias
Grammar: joining complex sentences using a wide range of conjunctions (S5)
Punctuation: commas and dashes (S7)
Writing features: features of encyclopaedia texts (T17; T24)

Reports
Information texts

Reports are used to describe or classify something. They usually begin with a general introduction to orientate the reader then move on to a description of particular characteristics and end with a summary. They often also include details of sources of further information and a bibliography to acknowledge sources of information.

The main difference between a report and a recount is that a report is usually non-chronological.

Report writing needs careful planning, use of research, logical organisation and editing skills. Children need to be made aware that when they are researching a subject and then writing it up, they are in fact writing a report on the information they have found out.

Illustrations and diagrams are often included to present information in a simplified form to clarify ideas.

Other features of non-chronological writing include the use of:

- an impersonal third person style;
- technical language;
- language to describe and differentiate;
- the present tense in most cases;
- the passive voice;
- linking words and phrases.

Understanding the technique of non-chronological writing in the third person is important for many areas of the curriculum.

Reports

Examples of information texts

www.henryandjoey.com about two pet pygmy goats by David Watts. Original version 1999 at age 12.

My Pet Kitten by Honor Head (Belitha Press) 2002

Snail by Chris Macro, Karen Hartley, Jill Bailey, 'Bug Books' series (Heineman library, 1999)

Horse and Pony Care Funfax (Dorling Kindersley, 1999)

Bats by Philip Richardson, 'Life' series (The Natural History Museum, 2002)

Raging Rivers by Anita Ganeri 'Horrible Geography' series (Schmidt Interactive Software Inc. paperback book, 2000)

The Cloud Book by Tomie de Paola (Holiday House, 1985)

A Visit to France by Peter Roop (Heinemann Library, 2000)

The children's illustrated version of the report is on page 6 of the resource book.

Pet Pygmy Goats[1]

General Information[2]

[3]Pygmy goats originally came from parts of <u>Africa</u>[4] – in particular from <u>Nigeria</u>[4] and <u>Cameroon</u>.[4] They are not completely white like many goats that are kept to produce milk. They can be brown, white with black or brown markings or many shades of grey and sometimes with a shade of blue. Some of the best looking pygmy goats have an attractive combination of several of these colours.

[3]These goats are very small: most are less than 60 centimetres from the ground to the top of the back of the goat. <u>Most</u>[5] have a barrel-shaped body with a fat stomach and quite short legs. They grow horns as they grow older although sometimes the horns are removed to make them safer as pets. A beard usually grows under the chin. There are also two small tassels called 'toggles' on the neck. A short tail is usually held up, looking rather like a flag! Females have udders that produce milk for baby goats, which are called 'kids'.

[3]<u>Some pygmy goats were taken from Africa to zoos in Britain, often to be kept in paddocks where children can stroke them</u>.[6] Their kids were often <u>sold</u>[7] as pets. Pygmy goats <u>make</u>[7] great pets. In some ways, these small goats are similar to dogs. Goats enjoy human company, and <u>will sit</u>[7] as close to a human as possible. They are very playful, frequently butting balls and running around. They also like to butt each other playfully.

Parts of a pygmy goat[8]

[9]

Parts of a pygmy goat

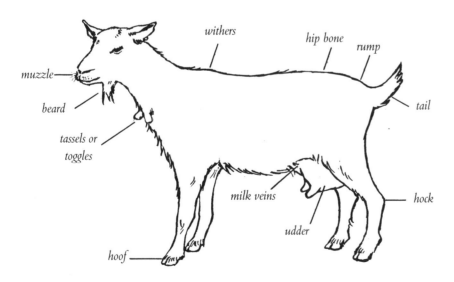

Food[10]

Goats do **not** eat everything they can find! They <u>may sniff</u>[11] and nibble at things, like clothes, but they certainly do not eat them! In fact pygmy goats can be quite fussy; for example, if a piece of dirt such as mud gets on their food, they will not eat it because it is dirty!

1. A big bold title makes it clear what the information is about.

2. A subheading for each section helps to divide the information and help the reader to find points of interest.

3. The first three paragraphs are written to orientate the reader and create a picture in the reader's mind of typical pygmy goats. The intention is to get the reader's interest by describing these attractive and amusing pet animals. Some historical details are given using the past tense. The third person is used throughout.

4. An initial capital letter is used for the names of continents and countries.

5. An example of a full stop at the end of a sentence and a capital letter at the beginning of the next sentence.

6. Suitable language for the reader – whether child or adult.

7. A verb. Without a verb the sentence does not make sense.

8. The diagram has a clear title.

9. Labels on a diagram make information very clear and easy to understand. A diagram can be used instead of a paragraph of description.

10. Another subheading, followed by a short paragraph.

11. Auxiliary verb and verb.

Pet pygmy goats <u>should</u>[12] be fed plenty of hay and a special goat mix which can be bought from shops that supply farmers. They also enjoy most vegetables that are eaten by humans. It is best to give small amounts of various types of leftover vegetables, such as carrots, along with plenty of hay. Eating too much of one type of food can cause bloat – a painfully swollen stomach. The goats love to eat treats such as the occasional biscuit but remember they are vegetarians!

Their food can be put in a bowl of the type used for feeding a large dog. It is best to put hay in a rack to keep it off the floor of the goat shed where it could get dirty. It is important to provide a mineral lick, which is a brick-sized solid lump of salt and other minerals, which the goats <u>will enjoy</u>[13] licking. This helps to keeps them healthy. Two or more water bowls (about the size of a washing up bowl) should be kept full and clean. They should be checked at least once a day and more often in hot weather. Smaller water containers are not a good idea because the goats will pick them up with their mouths, play with them and butt them!

They can be fed the goat mix once a day or it can be divided into two portions so they get it twice a day. They will soon get used to being fed at a particular time and <u>will bleat if you are late!</u>[14]

Goats will search for food to eat in their paddock, such as grass and leaves from trees. <u>They browse rather than graze. This means they bite off the best bits while walking around, rather than steadily eating grass like grazing sheep.</u>[15] Pygmy goats will eat garden flowers, particularly roses, <u>which can get them into trouble if they are not kept away from them!</u>[14] It is important to read about poisonous plants, perhaps in books in the library, to make sure you can recognise them and make sure goats do not eat them.

Shelter
<u>Pygmy goats need a place to sleep in at night and a paddock – an area of grass – to eat and move about on during the day</u>[16]. A simple shed will do for their night shelter and this is where their hay, water and other food should be put. They do not need a large field. An area large enough for them to run around and get exercise is sufficient.

<u>Pygmy goats are experts at escaping! They think this is great fun. It is not because they want to run away but because they are curious and want to explore ... and eat the roses!</u>[17] It is important to have a strong fence all round their paddock with a gate fastened with two bolts. They are clever animals and soon learn how to undo a bolt so they should be fitted where the goats cannot reach them. Thick wooden posts and rails are necessary; one and a half metres high. (They can jump high off the ground when feeling lively!) Strong wire netting called 'sheep wire' must be fixed to the wooden fence to keep them in. Pygmy goats do not like being <u>tethered</u>[18] (tied up using collar and lead) unless it is for only about fifteen minutes at a time and there is plenty of interesting food to eat!

They should have boxes and benches to sit and play on plus some balls they will like to butt around!

Goats also like each other's company. A pygmy goat must never be kept on its own. They are herd animals and one goat would be lonely and unhappy.

Health and care
Pygmy goats need their hooves trimmed regularly; otherwise they will start skidding everywhere! <u>To do this you need</u>[19] to tether the goat to a fence and give it some greenery to eat to take its mind off what is going on at the hoof-end of its body. Hoof trimming is like cutting toenails and does them no harm.

12 'Should' is a modal verb. Modal verbs are used to tell people to do things.

13 Future tense.

14 Use of humour to interest the reader.

15 Clarification of technical terms which may be unfamiliar to the reader.

16 Use of simple sentences makes important points easily understood so that there is no risk of ambiguity. Again a word that may be unfamiliar is explained.

17 Again, the use of humour.

18 Again a word that may be unfamiliar is explained.

19 The reader is addressed directly.

Pygmy goats will grow horns. Some goat keepers leave them to grow, but a horned goat, as a pet, can accidentally cause damage to people, fences and other goats. Many pygmy goats have their horn 'buds' removed by a vet when they are very young and before they start to grow horns. It is much more difficult for a vet to remove horns after they have grown.

In autumn the pygmy goat grows a thick fur coat and a layer of wool next to its skin. This keeps it warm enough not to need heating in its shed. After the winter the goat's coat moults, as the weather gets warmer. This makes it look very 'shaggy' and untidy for a time. It may be necessary to give the goat a shampoo to wash away the old coat and clean the skin. It is best and kinder to do this on a warm day. The goat should be tethered and fed with leaves to take its mind off the washing as it will not like it. It should be sprayed with a hose and a special animal shampoo used to get rid of any dandruff and loose hair. The shampoo should be rinsed off and the goat thoroughly dried with some old towels, trying not to let it chew the towels![20]

Pygmy goats are usually very healthy. They are normally lively, happy, bright eyed, frequently bleating, keen to feed, friendly to humans and, most of the time, their tails are held up higher than their backs, showing they are happy. (Except, of course, when feeling sleepy!) If a goat is not like this, it is important a vet is called to see it.

Your vet will advise on any forms to be completed for a government department, simple regular treatments to prevent worms in the stomach and annual vaccinations that are important to prevent some illnesses.[21]

20 More humour to enjoy. It helps the reader to imagine what the goat might get up to while being shampooed!

21 The reader is addressed directly again – this helps to add importance to the point that regular vet visits are recommended.

The above text is based on the website www.henryandjoey.com about
two pet pygmy goats by David Watts at the age of 12 in 1999.

Understanding the grammar and punctuation

Understanding the grammar and punctuation enables children to control the language they use and therefore to write effectively.

Grammar pointers

Verbs

Explain to the children that sentences cannot make sense without verbs. The verb refers to the action and can be described as the 'doing' word.

A sentence may have one main verb; for example:

> The pygmy goat <u>grows</u> a thick fur coat.

A sentence may have a main verb and an auxiliary verb; for example:

> ... which the goats <u>will enjoy</u>.

Tenses

The tense of a verb tells you when the action is taking place. There are three main tenses.

The **present tense** is used for what is happening now.

> They <u>think</u> escaping <u>is</u> great fun.

The **past tense** is used for what has happened.

> The pygmy goat breed <u>was</u> originally <u>found</u> in Africa.

The **future tense** is used for what is still to happen.

> Your vet <u>will advise</u> on some forms to fill in.

Auxiliary verbs are used to form different tenses. The most frequently used is from the verb 'to be'.

Punctuation pointers

Capital letters and full stops

Every sentence should begin with a capital letter and end with a full stop. Children often have problems deciding when to place the full stop. A sentence must be able to stand alone. It must make sense, otherwise it is just a sentence fragment. For example, the following sentence is not complete; we only have the beginning part of the information.

> Pygmy goats originally came from.

We need more information to complete the sentence.

> Pygmy goats originally came from parts of Africa – in particular from Nigeria and Cameroon.

> The children's version of these notes is on page 10 of the resource book.

Writing features
Organisational methods of report writing

Planning

Explain to the children how to research information using a variety of sources. Remind them how to make notes when researching and explain the importance of noting the source of the information in case it needs to be referred to again.

The information should then be organised and the writing planned. The intention is to make sure it is easy to read and in a sensible order so that it is easy to understand.

Many children will be inclined to write what they find most interesting at the beginning of their writing. This is to be encouraged up to a point, as it could make the introduction interesting and captivating. The introduction should also include general information giving some important facts.

Headings and subheadings

Discuss the use of headings and subheadings. Explain how these help the reader to find pieces of information and how they break up the text into sections that can be read and understood a section at a time. Pages of text with no headings are likely to cause readers to loose interest. A bold title will help to attract the reader's attention.

The children will probably be inclined to use short sentences with simple language and this is appropriate. There may be a tendency, though, to copy some long sentences from books and to include technical terms they do not understand. Point out that readers may not understand the technical terms either. If technical terms have to be used they should make it clear what the words mean. A brief explanation (perhaps in brackets) should be used.

> Eating too much of one type of food can cause bloat – a painfully swollen stomach.

> … provide a mineral lick, which is a brick-sized solid lump of salt and other foods …

> Pygmy goats do not like being tethered (tied up using a collar and lead).

Use of the third person

Explain how report writing uses the third person. It is important to make sure the children understand what is involved in writing in the third person. Explain that the first person refers to the person who is speaking or writing. An account written in the first person uses pronouns such as 'I', 'me', 'myself', 'mine', 'we', 'us', 'ourselves' and 'our'.

A third person account uses pronouns such as 'he', 'she', 'it', 'his', 'hers', 'they' and 'their'.

The difference can be illustrated:

> We feed them once a day.

becomes

> Goats can be fed once a day.

or

> They can be fed once a day.

Illustrations and diagrams

Diagrams and illustrations can be an important part of information texts. Diagrams need a clear title and labels. These draw attention to the parts of the illustration and clarify the accompanying explanation.

As well as drawing their own illustrations, the children can cut them out of newspapers, leaflets and magazines. Clipart is available from CD-Roms and the Internet, although it should not be over-used; there is a danger of the piece of work becoming a collection of colourful pictures!

Relevance and repetition

Remind the children to think about the title, subheadings and their planning to keep everything relevant. Much time can be wasted overdoing aspects on the fringe of the topic, such as lengthy detail on each breed of dog.

Avoid repetition. Some aspects of information shown on a diagram could be repeated in the text but one advantage of a labelled diagram is that it saves many words of explanation. The use of repetition to emphasise an important point or to summarise in a conclusion is permissible but should not be overdone.

Length

Reader boredom caused by including too much detail should be avoided.

> There are helpful hints for children on writing an information text on page 13 of the resource book.

Reports
Holiday guides

Holiday guides are non-chronological reports. Like information texts, they provide the reader with information about the subject, but they also usually have an element of persuasiveness in them. Many guides are written by people with great enthusiasm for the area being described or by people who have a commercial interest in it so they want to encourage people to visit it. Holiday guides therefore often have an overabundance of adjectives that praise the attractions and facilities being described. On the other hand, there can be versions designed to warn of the disadvantages of visiting an area but these are comparatively rare.

Devices for presenting text
Headings
Headings, subheadings and captions are used to break up the text and to draw the reader's attention to particular areas of the text. They help the reader to decide which parts to read in full.

Headings need to be eye-catching to stand out on the page. They are often in bold, clearly written lettering that is quick and easy to read.

Inset text
Inset text or text boxes can be used to vary the layout and create visual impact. There are usually only one or two per page and they are often in the form of a cation to a photograph or other illustration.

Lettering
Bold, italics and highlighted lettering can also improve the impact and variety of presentation but should not be overdone. A hierarchy of sizes and boldness helps to classify and categorise topics visually.

Illustrations
Charts, maps, photographs and sketches are very important to get the reader's attention. They save much description and tedious listing of facts and figures. They should have a clear title, caption and labels.

Reports

Examples of holiday reports

In and Around London for Kids by Judith Milling (Mainstream Publishing, 2001)

Usborne Handbook of France by Annabel Warrender (Usborne Publishing Ltd, 1992)

Birnbaum's Walt Disney World for Kids by Kids Ed. Wendy Lefkon, (Hearst publications, 1994)

Look Out London! by Louise Nicholson (Red Fox, 2000)

Devon & Cornwall by John Guy, 'Howling Monkey Short Break Guides' (Ticktock Media, 1999)

Discovering Ireland by Philip Steele (Zoe Books, 1996)

A Visitor's Guide to Ancient Rome by Lesley Sims 'Timetours' series, (Usborne Publishing Ltd, 1999)

A Cultural Guide to New York City for Kids, Families and Teachers by Patricia C Jones (Harry N Abrams Inc, 1998)

The children's illustrated version of the holiday guide is on page 20 of the resource book.

A Guide to The South Hams Area of Devon[1]

Location[2]

[3]The South Hams area is on the south coast of Devon, to the south of Dartmoor. It is between Plymouth and Torbay. The area includes a coastline with beautiful cliffs, sandy beaches and sheltered inlets. The beaches are some of the best in the country, often combining sand and rock pools with excellent scenery.

How to get there[2]

[3]The motorways M4 and M5 connect London with Devon and much of the midlands and north, via the M6. The A38 road continues from the M5 through Devon with turnings to the towns of South Hams.

Fast Intercity Express trains run to Devon from London and Birmingham many times a day. They stop at Exeter and Newton Abbot. The fastest service takes just over two hours from London to Exeter (St Davids).

There are also flights to Exeter and Plymouth airports.

[4]

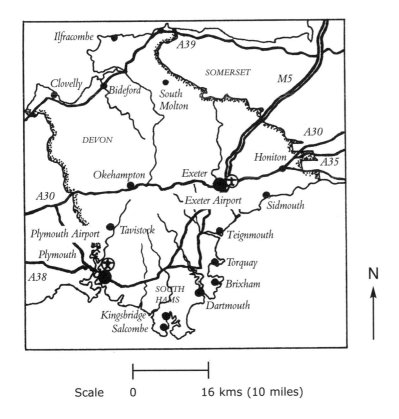

Scale   0   16 kms (10 miles)

1 Enlarged heading in bold print to make it clear what area the information is about.

2 Subheading for each section stands out clearly, divides up the information and helps the reader to find sections of particular interest.

3 The first two sections make it clear where the area is and how to get there. They aim to create interest so the reader will want to continue.

4 Maps present information and save detailed explanation, particularly if labelled fully.

[5]Typical Monthly Temperatures and Sunshine Hours For South Hams, Devon		
Month	Usual daytime temperature	Hours of sunshine
January	8	52
February	8	67
March	10	110
April	13	153
May	16	185
June	19	189
July	21	192
August	21	172
September	19	134
October	15	89
November	11	70
December	9	49

[6]Weather

This part of Britain has a good climate for holidays.[7] The weather can change at any time, as in all of Britain, but the following are the usual features of the area's weather:

- plenty of sunshine in the summer;
- temperatures usually quite warm in summer;
- the average number of days with no rain is high in the summer;
- winter is mild compared with many other parts of the country.[8]

The countryside

The countryside changes from the high, hilly moorland scenery to the north, to very green hills where cattle and sheep graze towards the south. In many places good views can be enjoyed over lush green farmland and out to the sea beyond. Ploughed fields have an unusual red colour because red sandstone colours the soil. Many country lanes are very narrow and run deep in cuttings worn into the sandstone by horse and carts before the roads were surfaced with tarmac. The towns and pretty villages have many interesting old buildings.

Places to visit include **Kingsbridge, Dartmouth, Totnes, Salcombe, Modbury, Hope Cove, Thurlestone** and **Torcross**.[9]

An unusual trip by tractor

An example of an interesting trip is the drive south to the town of **Bigbury on Sea**. The road winds[10] through very narrow deep cuttings and across lovely scenery to a beautiful beach near **Burgh Island**. This island is reached[11] at high tide by going on *a tractor ride*[12] across the beach and into the shallow sea at high tide. When the tractor drives[10] out of the sea onto the island's beach, visitors can reach the hotel and old Pilchard Inn on the island.

5 A chart is one way of presenting information clearly and briefly. It must have a clear title and headings for each column.

6 A chart should be followed by a caption or paragraph of explanation to make it relevant.

7 Words in italics stand out and therefore create greater emphasis.

8 Bullet points help to organise the information. They make the information stand out from the rest of the text. They also help to break up the page to make it look more interesting.

9 The use of words in bold lettering helps them to stand out from the text. This enables the reader to locate information more easily.

10 Most verbs in this type of non-chronological text are in the present tense.

11 The passive voice is used instead of 'We reach this island'.

12 Use of italics to emphasise the unusual aspect in this paragraph.

Some Places to Visit

<u>SALCOMBE</u>[13]

The town is a splendid sight in the summer. The green slopes of the South Hams hills make a background to the estuary full of white, tan and red sails. *Very attractive small, sheltered, sandy beaches nestle in rocky coves around the waterways.* These beaches are ideal for family days on the beach.

<u>The Museum of Maritime and Local History at Custom Quay in Salcombe shows how the town grew on its important shipping and yachting activities.</u>[14]

Everyone can find something to enjoy. The town has beaches, coastal walking, boating, varied shops in tiny side streets and a variety of restaurants and public houses. Salcombe is one of the main yachting centres in England. Many visitors arrive by boat and, in summer, there can be ten visitors for every local resident.

There are many hotels, guest houses and cottages to rent with *fascinating views of sea and scenery.* Some of the nearby caravan sites are *within easy reach of beaches.*

The Cookworthy Museum in the main street includes a reconstruction of an Edwardian chemist shop, a traditional farm and an outdoor gallery of farm equipment.

13 Headings can be varied and indicate a category by using different types of print. In this case, the use of capital letters for the names of towns to visit.

14 Inset text (centred in the page or in a box, and in smaller print) can separate out a particular type of information. In this case, information about museums.

KINGSBRIDGE

Kingsbridge is a busy market town inland from Salcombe and at the inland end of the fascinating channels and inlets of the sea reached from Salcombe.

Kingsbridge has many different types of shops, a cinema, a sports centre, an indoor heated swimming pool, bowls rink and nightclub. In the 13th century the Abbot of Buckfast Abbey gave permission for his monks to start an open-air market on the quay to sell their fruit, vegetables, thick cream and honey. There are still regular *weekly markets* on the quay.

There are many footpaths and country lanes for walker and cyclist access to the countryside with stunning scenery. There are plenty of pubs and inns along the routes providing lunch stops. Restaurants provide cream teas on the lawn.

There are plenty of hotels and breakfast farmhouses as well as cottages to rent for holidays. Campers and caravanners will find sites ranging from simple farm fields to touring parks with comprehensive facilities.

Attractions for all the family include National Trust properties, outdoor adventure parks with fair and wet weather facilities, farm attractions, riding, swimming, sailing, sail-boarding, golf, tennis, cycling, fishing, boat hire, and power-boating.

Excursions to other towns and cities

Larger towns and cities are less than an hour away from the South Hams area by car. **Plymouth** and **Exeter**[15] have theatres, cinemas and historical attractions such as Exeter cathedral.

The South Hams has fascinating small towns such as Dartmouth and Totnes but a short distance from here are the much larger towns of **Paignton** and **Torquay** which provide an interesting contrast with all the holiday amusements and entertainments of big seaside resorts.

The South Hams area provides a huge range of opportunities to enjoy on a holiday. These range from walks in the countryside, meals in restaurants in pretty villages and quiet boating activities, to the fun of a beach holiday and the nearby facilities of large holiday resorts and cities.[16]

---

15 Bold print is used to make it easier to find particular aspects. In this case the brief information on particular towns.

16 The final paragraph reminds the reader how good the area is for a holiday and emphasises the range of opportunities available for enjoyment.

Understanding the grammar and punctuation

Understanding the grammar and punctuation enables children to control the language they use and therefore to write effectively.

Grammar pointers

Verbs

Emphasise the importance of verbs in a sentence. The tense of a verb tells you when the action is taking place. There are three main tenses.

The past tense is used for what has happened.

The future tense is used for what is still to happen.

The present tense is used for what is happening now and the situation as it exists now.

> *There are many hotels, guest houses and cottages.*
>
> *Attractions for all the family include outdoor adventure parks.*
>
> *Many country lanes are very narrow.*

The present tense should be emphasised in connection with this type of non-chronological writing.

First and third person

It is important to make sure the children understand what is involved in writing in the third person. Explain that the first person refers to the person who is speaking or writing.

An account written in the first person uses pronouns such as 'I', 'me', 'myself', 'mine', 'we', 'us', 'ourselves' and 'our'.

A third person account uses pronouns such as 'he', 'she', 'it', 'him', 'her', 'they' and 'their'.

Punctuation pointers

Devices for presenting texts

Explain to the children how different types of lettering styles can be used to create different effects. For example:

✦ **Bold lettering** – used for headings and within the text to make the words stand out from the rest. This enables the reader to locate information quickly and easily.

> **How to get there**
>
> **Plymouth and Exeter have theatres...**

✦ **Capital letters** – also used to make words stand out on the page.

> **SALCOMBE**

✦ **Italics** – used to create emphasis on particular words within a text.

> There are still regular *weekly markets* on the quay.

✦ **Inset text** – this is used to add a caption to a picture or chart. The font is usually smaller than the rest of the text but it stands out because it is placed in an area on its own.

> The Museum of Maritime and Local History at Custom Quay in Salcombe shows how the town grew on its important shipping and yachting activities.

✦ **Headings and subheadings** – used to break up the text into sections so the reader can quickly scan the page to find what they are interested in.

> The children's version of these notes is on page 24 of the resource book.

Writing features
Gathering information and taking notes

Gathering information

Explain to the children that research means finding out about things and there are various ways of doing this:

✦ finding reference books/materials;
✦ searching CD-Roms;
✦ searching the Internet;
✦ interviewing people.

Children need to be shown how to find their way around these sources of information and the best way to use them.

When researching from books they should be aware of the following:

✦ **the contents page** – this lists the chapters, sections or units and may be the first source of retrieving information;
✦ **the index** – this is a list in alphabetical order of all the main topics mentioned in the book with relevant page numbers;
✦ **the glossary** – this is a dictionary of any special or technical words used in the book;
✦ **the bibliography** – as well as listing books referred to by the author, it will often give further reading material on the same subject. This is invaluable to the researcher.

When finding information, encourage the children to make their own notes and organise them under suitable headings. These can then be used as paragraph plans for their writing.

Taking notes

Explain to the children that when they are finding out information for a topic it is useful to be able to take notes quickly and efficiently. The purpose of note taking is to remind the writer of certain facts that he or she needs to include in his or her account without having to copy out laboriously details from the source material. It also helps to aid the writer to put the information in his or her 'own words' rather than copy the style of the source.

Notes are intended only for the person who is writing them; they should be as brief as possible but should be easily converted into information for others to read. The writer should be able to order his or her notes and expand on them in a logical manner.

When taking notes, the children may want to use the following methods:

✦ note the key words in sentences and paragraphs;
✦ use headings to order facts in a logical sequence;
✦ draw a web to organise facts;
✦ use acknowledged and invented abbreviations.

There are helpful hints for children on writing a holiday guide on page 27 of the resource book.

Instructions
Making or doing something

Instructions direct the reader to carry out a series of actions or steps in order to accomplish something. They can be oral, written, diagrammatic or a combination of those.

Simple instructional text speaks directly to the reader, using imperative verbs telling them to do this, then do that in sequential order so they can succeed in completing the task (hopefully).

Most children will have had experience of following simple instructional texts, such as how to play a game or complete a recipe, but they usually have less experience of writing instructions. It is important, then, that they have practical experience of the task they are writing instructions for before they actually set out to write the instructions.

Instructions are usually written in the imperative tense. Sequencing is important and they often include numbered steps and/or time connectives, such as first, then, now, next and finally.

Instructions need clear, concise language. Adjectives and adverbs need to be used in order to clarify things rather than to describe things.

Diagrams are used to make instructions more concise. They need to be clearly labelled.

Instructions

Examples of instructions for making or doing something

- ✦ Instructions for making things in design and technology
- ✦ Rules for sports and games
- ✦ Instructions for using equipment
- ✦ Care and maintenance instructions
- ✦ Cooking recipes
- ✦ Instructions on cans of paint and other consumable products
- ✦ Assembly instructions for many toys and gadgets
- ✦ First aid instructions
- ✦ Safety instructions
- ✦ How to use ICT equipment and software
- ✦ Knitting or sewing patterns

Books

Jazzy Jewelry to Make and Wear by Diane Baker (Williamson Publishing Co, 2001)

Making Jewellery Step by Step by Sara Grisewood (Kingfisher Books, 1999)

Papier Mâché Step by Step by Judy Balchin (Heineman Library, 2000)

How to Draw Horses by Lucy Smith (Usborne Publishing Ltd, 1993)

Children's Quick and Easy Cookbook by Angela Wilkes (Dorling Kindersley, 1997)

Dinner from Dirt: Ten Meals Kids Can Grow and Cook by Emily Scott (Gibbs M Smith Inc, 1995)

Watch It Grow for Young Gardeners by Ivan Bulloch (Two-Can Publishing, 2002)

Easy Peasy: Real Cooking for Kids Who Want to Eat by Mary Contini & Pru Irvine (Ebury Press, 1999)

The children's illustrated version of the instructions is on page 34 of the resource book.

How to Make a Paper Aeroplane[1]

The Classic Dart

These instructions are to help you make a paper aeroplane that is designed to fly really well. Changing the design will make it fly in different ways. It is fun to make one that does loops and rolls as it flies. After you have made it, try experimenting with other designs.[2]

Equipment and materials[3]

You will need: An A4 sheet of paper
You may also need: scissors

What to do[4]

[5]1. First[6] take a rectangular[7] sheet of paper and fold it down the centre dotted line. Open it out again afterwards. (Diagram 1)

2. Now fold the top left and right corners in to meet the centre line. (Diagram 2)

3. Fold the slanting top left- and right-hand edges in once more to lie along the centre line.[8] (Diagram 3a)

4. The result should look like Diagram 3b.

9

10

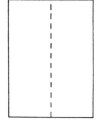
Diagram 1

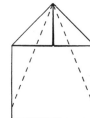
Diagram 2

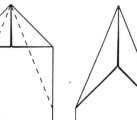
Diagram 3a **Diagram 3b**

1	A bold title makes the purpose of the instructions clear.
2	An introductory paragraph is designed to gain the reader's attention and make them want to read on.
3	Details of the equipment and materials needed are provided at the beginning of the instructions so the reader can get everything together before beginning.
4	Subheadings are used to help the reader locate easily the information required.
5	The layout of these instructions is a series of numbered sections and diagrams. The numbering indicates that there is a sequential order for making the plane.
6	Time connectives reinforce the sequencing.
7	An adjective is used to make the instruction more concise.
8	The use of the imperative verb addresses the reader directly. The imperative often comes at the beginning of the sentence.
9	Clearly labelled diagrams help the reader to follow the instructions more concisely.
10	Sometimes two diagrams are used to illustrate a more involved step in the instructions.

5. Now fold the plane in half along the centre line again, making sure it folds inwards. (Diagram 4a)

6. Seen from the side it will look as in Diagram 4b.

7. Fold the long slanting folded edge down to match the lower centre line edge. (Diagram 5a)

8. The result should look like Diagram 5b.

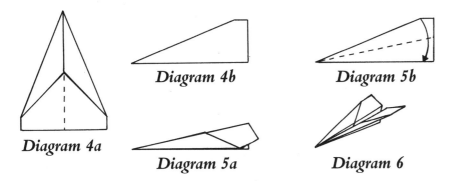

Diagram 4a

Diagram 4b

Diagram 5a

Diagram 5b

Diagram 6

9. Turn over and repeat.

10. Open out the wings to a slight upward angle when looking down the plane from the nose. (Diagram 6)

[11]Flying your plane
Throw slightly pointed upwards. Remember: DO NOT aim at people's eyes and faces – the point of the nose is very sharp![12]

Try to experiment with cutting flaps in the rear edge of the wings and adjusting them to alter the flight of the plane. You can make a flap by making two short parallel cuts in the rear edge and fold the paper between the cuts up or down.

Watch what happens when you fold the flaps down compared to up.

Watch what happens when you have different flaps on each wing.[13]

For further exciting designs go to: www.paperairplanes.co.uk[14]

11 Further instructions are provided for flying the plane once it has been made.

12 Important safety tips are mentioned.

13 The reader is encouraged to have fun with the end product and to experiment with the design.

14 The reader is provided with useful further information to develop the project further.

How to Row a Boat[1]

Rowing a boat can be very enjoyable. It provides a way of exploring parts of the countryside that can not be reached on foot. The sensation of gliding through the water is very different from walking or cycling. The exercise is also very healthy![2]

A major difference between rowing and cycling or walking is that when rowing you sit with your back to the direction you are travelling in. This makes it possible to use your weight to pull on the oars. It is important to look round quite often to make sure you know where you are going! Feet should be braced against the back of the boat or against a footstop (ledge) on the floor.

Equipment and clothing[3]
You will need: a boat, oars, lightweight clothing, rubber-soled shoes and a life-jacket.[4]

First attempts at rowing should be done slowly and carefully.[5]

There are four things to do which can be called stages of rowing:
1. Put the oar in the water.
2. Pull the oar through the water.
3. Lift the oar out of the water.
4. Get ready to do the movement again.[6]

[7]1. Put the oar in the water.

✦ The oar should be placed in the rowlock so that it balances well and rests on the water without sinking more than the blade below the water.

✦ Holding the handles of both oars, lean forward so that your nose is over your toes.

✦ Keep your head up. Prepare to put the blade in the water.[9]

Lean forward with your head up.[10]

2. Pull the oar through the water.

✦ Legs do most of the work at this stage. <u>Push with your feet against the floor or back of the boat</u>.[11] At the same time start pulling with your arms and back.

Pulling the oar provides the power to make the boat move.

✦ Keep your arms straight and swing your back from the hips. Pull the oar handle up to a position just below your chest.

✦ Do not dig the oar too deeply into the water. The blade should be just below the surface.

Pull the oar handle to just below the chest.

3. Lift the oar out of the water.

✦ At the end of the rowing stroke your back will be leaning slightly backwards.Take the blade out of the water quickly.

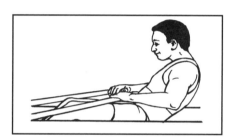

At the end of the stroke your back will be leaning slightly backwards

✦ **Important:** Take the oar out smoothly and ***quickly***[12] so that it does not get caught up with the movement of the water. Do this by lowering your whole arm: not just your wrists. If you are too slow and the oar blade gets dragged away, <u>the handle will push against your chest</u>[13] and could knock you to the floor or even overboard into the water! This is called 'catching a crab'.

4. Get ready to do the movement again.

✦ Practice makes perfect. You will probably be rather clumsy at first and things will go wrong. Remind yourself to do each of the four parts of the rowing movement in order and slowly at first. Soon the movements will become regular and routine so you will not have to think about it. The movement will become graceful and smooth. Speed can then be increased but remember to look where you are going!

✦ <u>A sense of achievement can soon be enjoyed as you glide smoothly through the water.</u>[14]

Things not to do[15]	**Things to do**
Do not leave the oar in the water at the end of a stroke.	Do look round often to see where you are going.
Do not dig the oar too deeply into the water.	Do start slowly and carefully.
	Do keep your head up.

11 The present tense is used in most of the sentences.

12 This word is in bold and italics to emphasise its importance.

13 The future tense is needed in some sentences.

14 A statement or paragraph at the end concludes by reminding the reader of the enjoyment to be had from this activity.

15 Final safety warnings are issued to make sure the reader carries out the instructions correctly.

Understanding the grammar and punctuation

Understanding the grammar and punctuation enables children to control the language they use and therefore to write effectively.

Grammar pointers

Verbs

Remind the children that a sentence must have a verb because it is concerned with the action taking place. Instructions are clearly full of actions.

The tense of a verb tells you when the action is taking place. There are three main tenses.

The **present tense** is used for what is happening now.

The **past tense** is used for what has happened.

The **future tense** is used for what is still to happen.

Instructions are usually written in the **imperative** tense. For example:

> _Lift_ the oar out of the water.

It may sometimes be appropriate to use the future tense to indicate what will or could happen as a result of what is being done. For example:

> _... the handle will push against your chest ..._

Using the second person

When children write instructions about an activity they have experienced there is the temptation to write in the first person, explaining their experiences rather than giving instructions. It is important to insist on the use of 'you' and 'your' to ensure the second person is used.

Another way to write instructions is to write 'one's' instead of 'your' and 'one' instead of 'you' as in the sentence below:

> _If one is too slow and the oar blade gets dragged away, the handle will push against one's chest and could knock one to the floor or even overboard into the water!_

It is unusual for this method to be used except in the most formal circumstances. Even royalty are less inclined to use it currently!

Adjectives

Adjectives are describing words. Children are familiar with using adjectives when writing descriptive prose but they need to be made aware that when writing instructions a more disciplined approach to their use is needed.

Adjectives used in writing instructions should be used only to make clear exactly what has to be done. They improve the clarity of the instructions – they are not intended to create a beautiful image in the mind of the reader or arouse emotions as they might in a piece of prose. For example:

> _First take a rectangular piece of paper..._

It is useful to collect examples of different types of instructions and use them to find sentences with adjectives in them. The sentences can then be rewritten without the adjectives. This will show how important they can be in making instructions clear and precise. Another technique is to replace the adjectives used with other adjectives to see what this would do to the meaning of the sentence.

There can be confusion between adjectives and adverbs, which modify verbs. It is worth pointing out that if the word is added to a verb rather than a noun it is an adverb and not an adjective. Adverbs are also used to clarify actions in instructions.

Punctuation pointers

Commas

Commas are used to make it easier for the reader to make sense of a sentence or list.

In a list the commas are used to separate the items in that list. It is not usual to place a comma before the 'and' but this can sometimes be appropriate. For example:

> _You will need: a boat, oars, lightweight clothing, rubber-soled shoes and a life-jacket._

> The children's version of these notes is on page 38 of the Resource book.

Writing features
Organisational features of instructions

Explain to the children that they will need to think carefully about who is to read the instructions and what the purpose of the instructions are.

The instructions should be organised with points arranged in sections. These sections can be organised in different ways:

✦ Chronological order
Starting with the first step and then proceeding sequentially until the item is made or the activity is completed.

✦ Order of importance
Beginning with the most important aspect and going on to the other stages in a logical sequence.

✦ Alphabetical order
There may be no particular or obvious order to the instructions so alphabetical headings can be used to help the reader find pieces of information more easily.

The children will need to decide which layout device to use. This will vary according to the audience and the type of instructions. The instructions could be set out as:

✦ Continuous writing.
✦ Subheadings with paragraphs.
✦ Subheadings with bullet points.
✦ A numbered or bulleted list of points.
✦ Numbered subheadings with paragraphs.

Continuous writing

This is the most difficult way to set out instructions. It is harder for the reader to follow the instructions because it is easier to lose your place than in instructions with clearly defined subheadings.

Subheadings with paragraphs

Short paragraphs under clear headings give the opportunity for more detail to be included. The headings make it clear where to find information.

Numbered or bulleted list of points

It is easier to follow instructions when they are laid out clearly in points. When the activity involves making something the numbered step-by-step organisation avoids confusion.

Numbered subheadings with paragraphs

This method combines the best aspects of the others, particularly where there is a clear sequence to be followed.

The instructions can be helped to flow more smoothly with **time connectives** such as:

firstly, secondly, next, after this, the next stage

Illustrations/diagrams

Diagrams make instructions more concise. Depending on the artistic abilities of the children, they could draw their own, use computer clipart or cut pictures from old magazines. The diagrams need to be clearly labelled and can include suitable captions. A diagram without any labels does not provide much information and will only decorate the page. Photographs can also be included. There are several computer programmes that can be used to place photographs and labels.

An **introduction** to the subject is usually appropriate, indicating what will be covered. In the case of each of the example texts, there are attempts to make the processes sound appealing and enjoyable.

In the same way, a **conclusion** will round off the writing. A main point to include is that something worthwhile will have been achieved. Referring back to the introduction helps. Consideration of what could happen next can be included.

Depending on the activity, a text box containing a list of things to do and not to do could be included. This feature is often used when aspects of safety are to be emphasised.

There are helpful hints for children on writing instructions on page 41 of the resource book.

Instructions
Directions

Directions are a form of instructions – they tell people how to arrive at a particular destination from a certain starting point. Like all instructions, accuracy is the most important aspect – they need to be given in a particular sequence and include all the important detail in order for them to be followed successfully. We have all at some time experienced the frustration and time-wasting ordeal of receiving poor quality and misleading directions!

Giving good directions requires some geographical knowledge and the ability to give instructions clearly. Children may have little experience of giving or following directions so it is important that they learn to write in a structured and logical manner. Using step-by-step procedures children can, with the careful use of grammar, maps and diagrams, write directions that are effective, useful, clear and concise.

A useful exercise is to collect examples of directions. Examples that could be tried are a route planner on a computer and publication by motoring organisations. These can be used as a source of ideas and perhaps, illustrations, for their own writing.

The successful directions writer needs to:
✦ be aware of how much the reader will already know about the situation before he begins so that he can target his directions according to his audience;
✦ have a thorough understanding of how to get from place A to place B in order to be able to visualise it in detail;
✦ put himself in the place of the person who is trying to use the directions;
✦ check that his directions follow a logical sequence and are unambiguous;
✦ keep terminology to the minimum and fully explain unfamiliar terms;
✦ use straight forward, clearly labelled diagrams.

Instructions

Examples of direction texts

Route planners on the Internet:
http://www.theaa.com/travelwatch/planner_main.jsp
http://www.rac.co.uk/
http://routeplanner.lycos.co.uk/
http://www.viamichelin.com/viamichelin/gbr/dyn/controller/HomePage

An unusual version is the route planner for travelling by canal:
http://www.mihalis.net/canal/cgi-bin/canal.cgi

Routes can also be found in publications by the AA and RAC.
There are many road atlases available including the well-known A to Z series.
Large scale Ordnance Survey maps can be borrowed from local libraries.
Most libraries have a section on the local area including books giving directions for walks.
Tourist information offices have publications giving directions to many places of interest, often in free leaflets with maps and diagrams.
www.walkingworld.com is a website devoted to directions for walking routes.

Very useful sources of maps are the websites:
www.streetmap.co.uk/
www.multimap.com

The children's illustrated version of the directions is on page 48 of the resource book.

Directions to the Fairground near Thorpe Park[1]

Directions from the park to the fairground for someone who knows the area[1]

Map 1[2]

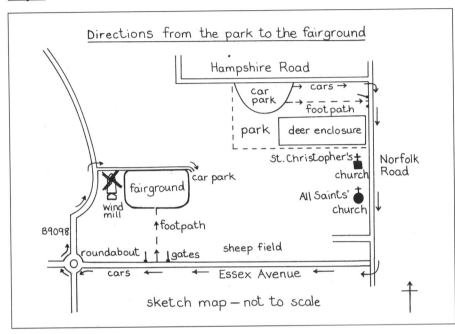

Directions from the park to the fairground

Hampshire Road

sketch map — not to scale

[3]

1. Go out of the park through the big gate near the end of the deer enclosure.
2. Turn right.[4]
3. Walk past the two churches and take the second turning on the right.
4. Walk along this road past the field where sheep are sometimes grazing.[5]
5. When you get to a pair of iron gates on the right, go through them on to the footpath.
6. The fairground is at the end of the footpath.

[6]**Directions from the park to the fairground for someone who does not know the area**

1. This is a large park and it is very easy to get lost so be careful to walk along the footpath beside the fence round the deer enclosure, until you get to a big gate.[7]
2. Go[8] out of the park through this gate.
3. Turn[8] right and walk along Norfolk Road.
4. 300 metres[9] along Norfolk Road there is St Christopher's Church. Walk past it.
5. Another 200 metres along the road is another church called All Saints' Church. Walk past this church too.
6. Take the SECOND turning on the right, which is Essex Avenue.
7. Walk along this road past the field where sheep are sometimes grazing.[10]
8. Look out for a pair of iron gates at the start of a footpath. Go through these gates onto the footpath.
9. Walk about 100 metres along the footpath and you will see the fairground at the end of this footpath.

1 Bold print makes the title and subheading stand out and makes the purpose of the directions clear.

2 A simple, clearly labelled sketch map makes the directions very much easier to follow.

3 The layout is a series of short, numbered sentences and phrases, producing a list that should be easy to follow.

4 The reader is addressed directly.

5 Landmarks are indicated to assist with orientation.

6 This brings out the substantial differences between the directions for someone who knows the area and directions for someone who does not. This version is much more detailed.

7 A considerate approach is required bearing mind the intention is to be as helpful as possible.

8 The use of the imperative form of the verb tells the reader clearly what to do. This type of verb usually comes at the beginning of the sentence.

9 Approximate distances help to give scale to the directions.

10 The present tense is used for directions in most cases although the future tense may also be used.

Directions for a car driver[11]

1. Drive out of the car park and turn right onto Hampshire Road.
2. At the end of the road turn right[12] onto Norfolk Road.
3. A short distance along this road you will pass the park gates on the right and you will see two churches.
4. When you get to the second church, which is All Saints' Church, you will see two right turnings.
5. Turn into the second turning, which is Essex Avenue.
6. Drive along this road past the field where sheep are sometimes grazing.
7. Drive past a pair of iron gates on the right. DO NOT DRIVE THROUGH THEM[13] because this is a footpath and not a road.
8. 200 metres further on there is a roundabout.
9. Take the third exit at the roundabout so you turn right onto the B9098[14] road.
10. This road curves round to the right and as it becomes straight again there is a windmill on the right.
11. Turn right into the track beside the windmill.
12. 300 metres along the track you turn right into the fairground car park.

Long distance directions
Driving directions from Basingstoke to Thorpe Park theme park

[15]**From Basingstoke:**

Road[16]	Direction[17]	Details	Distance[18]	Minutes[18]
A30	East	Towards Hook	8km	10
M3	North east	At Junction 5	23km	14
M3 onto A322	North	At Junction 3		
		Past Bagshot	2km	2
A30	North east	Through Sunningdale	8km	8
B389	East	Past Virginia Water	4km	4
A320	North east	To THORPE PARK on left.	2km	3
			Total 47 kilometres	Total 41 minutes

Map 2[19]

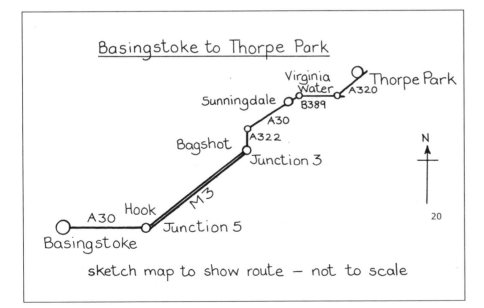

Basingstoke to Thorpe Park

sketch map to show route – not to scale

20

11 This is another version for a different purpose. It helps to show that directions have to be written precisely for the circumstances of the reader: in this case a car driver.

12 Left and right are used. Compass directions could also be included when this helps.

13 Important information is made to stand out by using capital letters.

14 The directions for car drivers need added information such as road numbers.

15 A chart in the form of a table of columns and rows organises the directions particularly clearly for a driver who can only glance at them when driving.

16 Bold, clear lettering also makes it easy for a driver to read quickly and safely.

17 Compass directions are helpful as well as the road numbers, motorway junction numbers and place names that appear on signposts.

18 Details of the distance and time to travel each section of the route helps to prepare the driver for the next change of direction.

19 A sketch map diagram of the route is clearer to follow than a map with too much detail.

20 It is important to indicate the direction of north when compass directions are used in the written directions.

Understanding the grammar and punctuation

Understanding the grammar and punctuation enables children to control the language they use and therefore to write effectively.

Grammar pointers

Plurals

A noun is a naming word. When there is more than one of something we use the plural form of the noun – usually by adding an 's'. Some examples are:

Singular	Plural
one metre	200 metres
one minute	41 minutes
one kilometre	ten kilometres
one gate	two gates
one turning	two turnings

Some plural rules

If a noun ends with s, x, z, sh or soft sounding ch you add 'es'.

church	churches
buzz	buzzes

If a noun ends with a 'y' and has a consonant before it, you change the 'y' to 'i' then add 'es'.

baby	babies
fly	flies

If a noun ends with 'f' or 'fe' you normally change the 'f' or 'fe' to a 'v' then add 'es.

calf	calves
knife	knives

Remind the children that there are always exceptions to these rules!

Some nouns have an irregular plural form; for example:

tooth	teeth
child	children
ox	oxen
woman	women

Some nouns are the same in singular and plural forms, for example:

deer, sheep, aircraft, trout, salmon, moose

Some nouns appear in the plural form only, for example:

cattle, binoculars, pyjamas, shorts, jeans, scissors

Punctuation pointers

Capital letters

As well as reminding the children of the importance of a capital letter at the start of every sentence, the more complex area of their use within a sentence should be covered. This includes the use of capitals for the first letter of titles and names, such as for people, days of the week, countries, places, religions and organisations, and for many abbreviations and capital letters used in the titles of books, articles and headings for paragraphs and diagrams.

titles and names; for example:

Mr. David Watts

days of the week, for example:

Monday, Tuesday, Wednesday

countries, places, for example:

England, Wales, Scotland, Northern Ireland
London, Cardiff, Edinburgh, Belfast

religions, for example:

Christianity, Hinduism, Islam

organisations, for example:

St. Christopher's Church

titles of books, for example:

The Holy Bible

abbreviations, for example:

MP (for Member of Parliament) and Co. (Company).

When a new line of poetry is started a capital letter is used for the first word.

Capital letters can be used to emphasise particular words so that they are seen as more important than other words; for example:

Take the SECOND turning on the right, which is Essex Avenue.

Drive past a pair of iron gates on the right. DO NOT DRIVE THROUGH THEM because this is a footpath and not a road.

The children's version of these notes is on page 51 of the resource book.

Writing features
Organisational features of directions

Planning

Explain how to research the necessary information using a variety of sources. There are plenty of maps of various types as well as publications by motoring organisations. Websites also have route planners and tourist information, including walking routes. The information should be organised and the writing planned. The intention is to make sure it is easy and quick to read, in a logical order and is easy to understand.

A **bold title** should be used to make it clear what the information is about.

Many children will be inclined to write as if the person requiring the directions already knows the area. It is important to emphasise the instructions should be for someone who does not know the area. In this way they are encouraged to make the directions more detailed.

If possible, it would be valuable to walk a route within the school grounds or further afield and make notes of directions along the way.

Devices for presenting text

A page of text is not the easiest format to follow when using directions. The layout should be more like a list of points with each stage separated.

The children can be encouraged to experiment with various ways of presenting the directions. They could discuss with each other what style they find easiest to follow. In the case of directions for a car driver a chart or table may be considered the most helpful layout. Large print in a chart is much easier to read than plain text. It separates the various items clearly and can be read comparatively safely, at a glance.

The use of titles in the largest, darkest print or capital letters and headings in bold but less prominent print should be explained. The children should be encouraged to find examples of ways in which lettering for directions is presented. They may, quite justifiably, criticise the size of print and layout of directions given in some route planners. Capital letters, enlarged or italicised print and headings can then be used.

Diagrams and maps

Maps, or at least sketch map diagrams, are a very important aspect of writing directions. Establish the important principle that a diagram must have a clear title and labels. These draw attention to the parts of the diagram and clarify the accompanying explanation. To be geographically correct, a map should also have a scale (or 'Sketch Map, not to Scale' should be added), a key to the symbols used and an arrow showing the direction of north.

There are helpful hints for children on writing directions on page 54 of the resource book.

Note taking

Note taking is a skill needed in many areas of the curriculum and in many walks of life. It is important to be able to take notes quickly and effectively. The notes remind the writer of relevant facts that need to be included in an account, such as writing up research, or be remembered for a particular purpose, such as giving a speech. It is vital, then, that the notes make sense to the writer after they have been completed!

Notes need to be brief but also arranged in a logical sequence so that they can be easy to understand. It is useful to use abbreviations and other shortened forms of writing, such as symbols and diagrams. Text messaging has created a new abbreviated written language that children may find useful in their note taking.

But perhaps the first rule of note taking is to be clear at the outset about what kind of information or ideas you need to record. Notes need to be focused – what angle or interest are you pursuing? Why are you taking the notes? How will they be used?

The biggest difficulty children have in taking notes from books or internet sources lies in the temptation to copy out huge chunks of text! They need help in learning how to read the information, understand what it means and then write out the main points in their own words. This takes lots of practice.

Underlining or highlighting the main ideas is a useful way of summarising sentences and paragraphs.

Once the main ideas have been identified, they need to be organised in some way. Subheadings are useful to divide the information into suitable sections and will help the writer find the information again when it is needed. Lists and diagrams such as charts and spider diagrams are also very useful summarising tools.

It is vital to make a bibliography of the sources used to make the notes. This saves a great deal of time if the notes need expanding or verifying at a later date. It is very frustrating if you can't remember where you got the information from!

Note taking

Examples of sources for understanding how to take notes

http://www2.ntu.ac.uk/sss/support/studyskills6notes

http://www.memory-key.com/StudySkills/notetaking

http://www.memory-key.com/StudySkills/notetaking_examples.htm

http://www.sas.calpoly.edu/asc/ssl/notetaking.systems.html

http://www.familyeducation.com/printables/package/1,2358,23-28245,00.html

http://www.iss.stthomas.edu/studyguides/booknote.htm

The Mind Map Book by Tony Burzan (BBC Consumer Publishing, 2000)

The children's illustrated version of the information and notes is on page 61 of the resource book.

King James I and the Gunpowder Plot [1]

The first Stuart king: King James I [1]

King James was born in 1566 and was a baby when he became king of Scotland. Helpers, called regents, helped him to rule while he was a child.

As a boy, James [2] was often unwell and had a weakness of the legs. Even though it was difficult, he learned to ride a horse and became very good at it. While he was small he had to be tied on to the saddle so he did not fall off.

He was well educated and was particularly interested in religion. When he became a teenager he started making decisions himself and ruling as a real king.

When the English Queen Elizabeth I died in 1603, James became King James I of England as well as King James VI of Scotland. He said the countries must be called Great Britain, although many people did not like this. Something many people **did** like was his new version of the Bible which was much easier to understand. It is called 'The King James Version' of the Bible.

While king of Scotland from a baby, James was nearly 37 when he became king of England. He had pale blue eyes, an untidy thin brown beard, brown hair and thin legs. He was not very tall and looked fat because his clothes were bulky. There was a lot of material in his clothes to try to protect him against being stabbed by daggers if he was attacked.

James's tongue was too big for his mouth. This made it difficult for him to drink and the drink spilled out of his mouth making a mess. He never washed his hands; he just rubbed them on a cloth.

The Gunpowder Plot – 5th November 1605 [3]

Many people who were Catholics hated King James because he preferred the Protestant religion (The Church of England). Nowadays, we can pray to any god and be in any religion but 400 years ago people were told by the king or queen that they must pray in the way set out by the Church of England. James was the leader of the Church of England and he punished people who wanted to be Catholics.

Some Catholics were so angry that they got together and decided to kill him. Robert Catesby was their leader. Guy Fawkes was a Catholic soldier who knew how to use gunpowder. They decided to blow up the Houses of Parliament when the king was there. Barrels of gunpowder were secretly put into a cellar under the Houses of Parliament. They then waited for King James I to arrive. Guy Fawkes was to be the one to set light to the gunpowder – but it all went wrong.

Someone found out about the plot. A letter was sent to Lord Monteagle warning him not to go to the Houses of Parliament. He showed the letter to the king. Soldiers were sent to search the cellars. They discovered Guy Fawkes with matches ready to light the gunpowder. He was arrested and put in prison in the Tower of London. The other plotters rushed away on horseback but were caught and shot by the king's soldiers.

Guy Fawkes was later tortured and executed.

1 Clear headings and subheadings to show a note-taking reader exactly what the content consists of.

2 Use of a comma to indicate a pause.

3 Subheadings break up the text and can draw the attention when scanning text to write notes.

The people who liked James celebrated the failure of the gunpowder plot by making a dummy that looked like Guy Fawkes and burning it on a huge bonfire. Since then, every year on November 5th, there have[4] been celebrations with bonfires and fireworks.

Notes on this information

James I[5]
Born 1566 & King of Scotland as baby
Poor health but good horse rider & studied religion[6]
1603 also became king of Eng 37 yrs old
J[7]: new Bible version
thin beard, blue eyes, thin legs[8]
Looked fat because clothes too big for him
Tongue too big so messy drinker

Gunpowder plot
J punished Catholics so they hated him
Some plotted to kill J
Nov[9] 5th 1605 Robert Catesby & Guy Fawkes put gunpowder under parliament[10]
J found out
Soldiers caught GF[11]
GF[11] executed; other plotters shot
Bonfire celebrations still happen every 5th Nov

Spider Diagram of Notes on King James I[12]

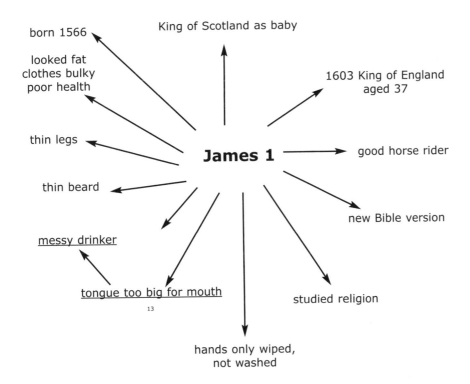

4   Commas used to indicate pauses and break up a sentence.

5   A heading used at the top of a column or list of notes.

6   Statement much reduced from the original text partly by deleting words.

7   Abbreviation used for James which should be obvious to any reader of the notes.

8   Commas to separate items in a list.

9   Abbreviation used for November.

10   Sometimes a complete phrase or two must be noted to keep the meaning.

11   GF initials used for Guy Fawkes after his full name has been used earlier in the notes. Initials are an acceptable form of abbreviation in note-taking.

12   An alternative method for making notes with more visual impact.

13   In some cases there may be links between notes on the diagram. In this case the arrow indicates a cause and effect without using words.

Flow diagram of notes on the Gunpowder Plot[14]

J punished Catholics

They hated him

|

Some plotted to kill J

|

Nov. 5th 1605

Robert Catesby & Guy Fawkes

put gunpowder under parliament

|

J found out

|

Soldiers caught GF – executed

others shot

|

Bonfire celebrations every 5th Nov

14 A flow diagram is an effective method for notes arranged as a sequence of connected events.

The main points are very clearly arranged as a type of list.

This layout provides spaces to write in information from other sources and to insert words when writing the first draft of an expanded version of the information.

Understanding the grammar and punctuation

Understanding the grammar and punctuation enables children to control the language they use and therefore to write effectively.

Grammar pointers

Deleting words and retaining meaning

When making notes, it is important for the children to identify words that are essential to the meaning of a sentence, so that the meaning is retained. They need to be able to identify nouns and verbs that must be retained while removing most qualifying words, adjectives, adverbs and many pronouns. Descriptions and sequences of events can be reduced to lists or diagrams. Numbers can replace words.The use of abbreviations that are not acceptable in other circumstances is acceptable in writing notes. For example:

> <u>James</u> was the leader of the Church of England and he <u>punished</u> people who wanted to be <u>Catholics</u>.

could become:

> J punished Catholics

Explain to the children how highlighting or underlining can be used to pick out the important words in a text. They can also be encouraged to experiment with deleting words using a word processor, on a white/blackboard, on OHP transparencies or by cutting up paper strips on which sentences have been written.

Punctuation pointers

Commas

Commas are used to make it easier for the reader to make sense of a sentence or list.

Commas show the reader where to pause for a moment. They can be useful in more complicated sentences where they break up the sentence and make it easier to understand.

> *Helpers, called regents, helped him to rule while he was a child.*

A comma is used to separate items in a list.

> *thin beard, blue eyes, thin legs*

Once the children decide to use commas they can sometimes get too enthusiastic and overdo it! The rule to remember is to use a comma to indicate a pause where it helps to convey the meaning of the sentence. Do not use a comma where it does not help.

> The children's version of these notes is on page 64 of the resource book.

Writing features
Taking notes

Explain to the children that when they are collecting information from books, magazines and newspapers for a project, it is important to be able to take notes quickly and effectively. The purpose of note-taking is to remind the writer of relevant facts that need to be included in an account. This makes it unnecessary to copy out lengthy details from the original sources, which may, in any case, not be available at the time of writing the final work.

Notes are often intended only for the person writing them but they can be an abbreviated form of communication for other people.

Notes should be brief but understandable. They should be arranged in a logical sequence.

Some stages for making notes from a book:

1. Look through the pages quickly (scan them). If there are subheadings write them down as a framework. Alternatively, read the first one or two sentences of each paragraph. This should provide a rough outline.

2. Look at the topics noted and cross out any that are not important.

3. Write the main points as you read through.

4. Underline or highlight the main points.

5. Write notes using abbreviations and your own type of shorthand. Leave out details, descriptions and full explanations. Concentrate on the main points. Decide if a chart or diagram will help to summarise the points.

6. Keep bibliographic record of sources so you can refer back to them a later date if necessary.

Show the children a variety of methods for note taking including the listing of key words, the use of headings, subheadings and diagrams, such as a spider diagram or flow diagram, and the use of 'for' and 'against' columns or matrices.

An example of a spider diagram:

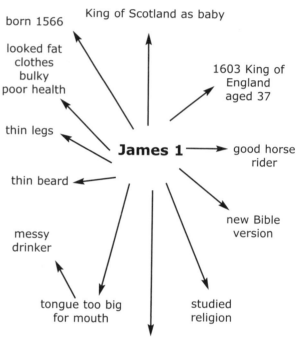

There are helpful hints for children on taking notes on page 67 of the resource book.

Recounts
Informal letters

Letters are a form of recount. Personal, informal letters retell events from the point of view of the person writing the letter. They are usually written in the past tense in the first person. They often use time connectives such as 'last week', 'next week' and 'when we arrived' to help structure the recount chronologically.

The writing of letters and messages is an ancient skill that could be lost in view of the vast increase in the use of email and text messages by telephone. It is a pity that far fewer letters are now written when one considers that the letter was the main form of full written expression the majority of people would use during their lives after leaving school. Now speed and brevity has taken over, it is important to establish the skills of full expression in letter form so the style can be used on paper and when time permits, in the body of an email.

Over recent centuries, the development of postal services and increased literacy made it possible for people to communicate by letter. This ability, along with transport developments, made letter writing a favourite pastime and the main method of keeping in touch with friends and family.

Writing a letter provides a way to express personal style whilst conveying thoughts, opinions and ideas effectively and concisely. The letters pages of newspapers flourish on individuals expressing themselves.

Most children will, at some stage in their lives, still need to write letters. These are, perhaps, more likely to be formal letters as covered in unit seven but an informal letter to a relative or close friend would need to be written in a warm and friendly style, quite different from the business letter or letter to complain. Within this type of letter writing there are differences between writing to friends of a similar age and writing to a grandparent who may not understand slang and fashionable expressions used by children. Standard English would have to be used and the tone of the letter changed appropriately.

One of the main attractions of writing letters is the enjoyable aspect of receiving a reply!

Recounts

Examples of informal letters

Letters from a Mouse by Herbie Brennan (Walker Books, 2001)
The Father Christmas Letters by J R R Tolkein (Harper Collins, 2000)
Skinny Melon and Me by Jean Ure (Collins, 2002)
The Deathwood Letters by Hazel Townson (Red Fox, 1991)
Dear Daniel: Letters from Antarctica by Sara Wheeler (Hodder Wayland, 1997)

Websites

http://www.askoxford.com/betterwriting/emoticons/
http://englishplus.com/grammar/00000143.htm

The children's version of the letter is on page 74 of the resource book.

A letter to a friend

246 Stickleback Walk
Smallstream
SS98 7AZ[1]

17/8/03[2]

Dear Praful[3]

We've just got back from a really good holiday.[4]

I wanted to go to another country for a holiday but Dad said we can't afford that until next year. Now I'm glad we stayed in England and went to the Norfolk Broads. I thought it would be boring living on a boat for two weeks. Who would want to do that for a holiday?[5] As it turned out, it was great fun.

Our car broke down on the way there. The AA man had to tow us to a garage at Wroxham. Then we had to carry all our luggage half a mile to the boat yard. Mum was quite cross and tired when we got there so Paul and I kept quiet. Dad, as usual, was quite cheerful. He said we would have a good time and the car would be repaired in time to go home.[6]

The boat looked small but when we got inside it there was quite a lot of room – except Dad banged his head on the roof and said some naughty words! I rushed into the boat and got the best cabin. Paul didn't like that and hit me. You know what he's like.[7] He's about as annoying as a brother can be at times.

The man from the boatyard showed us how to steer the boat. I was on top of the cabin and only just got down in time to go under a bridge! I thought, 'At least I hadn't fallen in on the first day.'

When we set off there were lots of boats on the river. Some of the people on them seemed very happy and couldn't steer straight. One boat went into the bank and got jammed in the branches of a tree.[8]

We went to a big lake called a 'broad'. It seemed a good idea to moor beside the reeds. I jumped off the boat with the mooring rope. I thought I was going to land on hard ground. But guess what?[10] It was mud! I sank in the mud up to my knees. Mum had to reverse the boat to pull me out of the sticky, black, smelly stuff.[11] I slid into the water on the end of the rope and pulled myself up onto the boat. I _had_ fallen in on the first day! It's a good thing there was a shower on the boat so I could clean the mud off myself. But the mud blocked the drain hole and Dad had to unblock it![9]

After Mum had calmed down, things went quite well for several days. We had lots of sunny weather. We had a rowing boat we towed behind. At one place where we moored, we took the rowing boat out to row to a village. The village church had a tower we could go up. We climbed up a long, dark, winding, spiral stairway. Paul kept clapping his hands loudly to hear the echo. He got told off by the vicar![12] At the top I felt excited and scared at the same time.[13] We could see a long way, right to the distant horizon, but there was a sheer drop right in front of us! The people below looked like ants. I wanted to throw a paper aeroplane over the side but Dad stopped me. He said it would annoy the vicar again and make litter. I sometimes think Dad wants to stop me

1 Own address in top right-hand corner.

2 Date is written informally.

3 Recipient of letter on next line next to the margin.

4 Informal friendly language and style.

5 Asking a rhetorical question involves the reader in the thoughts of the writer.

6 Some indications of the characters of her parents are given.

7 Involving the reader through familiarity with the brother he knows.

8 Some quite short sentences with impact and some implication that there were people enjoying themselves in various ways.

9 Use of an anecdote to add interest and humour to the letter.

10 A question to encourage the reader's anticipation and involvement.

11 Some vivid description to bring the story to life.

12 More about the brother gives an insight into aspects of his character.

13 Expression of feelings make the anecdote more interesting.

having fun because his dad stopped him doing fun things when he was a boy. Is your dad like that?[14]

When we got back to the rowing dinghy, Paul stepped on its side and it tipped up suddenly. He went head first into the water, scaring the ducks. This was really funny but it also meant we had to go straight back to the boat with my drippy[15] brother instead of having an ice cream.

The next day it rained and was very windy. Some children on another boat asked us to go onto their boat and do some fishing. I caught a fish called a pike, which had lots of sharp teeth in its big mouth.[16] I wanted to keep it to cook for a meal but the girl on the other boat said that's cruel. I said it's a cruel fish because it eats other fish and it tried to bite me. She grabbed it and threw it back. So I pushed her in after it.[17]

The next day[18] was boring because I had to stay in my cabin all day as a punishment.

When Mum and Dad had calmed down things improved, the weather got sunny again and we went a long way on the boat to visit interesting places. Mum and Dad even let me steer the boat. Have you ever steered a boat? It is exciting and strange. The boat turns a long time after you turn the wheel. Not like a car. It took some time to get used to it. I missed hitting the bridge though and other boats were quite good at getting out of my way.

Dad managed to avoid mooring at big towns because he said it would be busy and noisy to stay near a town. I think it was because he didn't want Mum to disappear all day in the shops.[19]

In the last few days[18] we set off back towards the boatyard. We made friends with a family on another boat going in the same direction. They were in a big old sailing boat, which also had a motor. I went on their boat for a day. Using the sails was great fun. When the wind was strong the boat leaned right over and we went faster than the motorboats. That family got on well with my mum and dad and they invited us to go on their boat with them for a weekend in September. Would you like to come too?[20]

When we got back[18] to the boatyard our car had been repaired so we were able to go home in it. Mum had taken a while to get used to the boat but she ended up enjoying the holiday even more than Dad. She is very keen for us to buy our own boat if we can ever afford it.[21] Can you imagine it? Going out in a boat whenever we want to. Fantastic![22] Perhaps we won't go abroad next year so we can afford to buy our own boat on the Norfolk Broads.[23]

I'm looking forward to seeing you to tell you lots more.[24]

See you soon,[24]

Helen

PS. If we buy a boat you could come out on it with us. HP

14 Draws the reader into the letter by asking a question.

15 Occasional use of informal language. Humour and slang is appropriate in this informal letter.

16 Description helps to create interest and provide enjoyment for the reader.

17 Honesty and frankness about misbehaviour, appropriate to a friend, but not to an adult who may disapprove.

18 Time connective.

19 Provides an amusing insight into her parents.

20 Another question and one that will encourage the recipient to write a letter in reply.

21 More indication of Mum's character and an unexpected development.

22 A question to draw the reader into the letter by addressing him directly.

23 Brings the letter full circle, back to the comments at the start of the letter and looks to the future.

24 Casual and friendly signing-off.

Understanding the grammar and punctuation

Understanding the grammar and punctuation enables children to control the language they use and therefore to write effectively.

Grammar pointers

Pronouns

Pronouns are words used in place of nouns. They are naming words that are usually shorter than the nouns they replace. They may refer to things: it, this, that, those.

> *The boat looked small but when we got inside it there was quite a lot of room.*

Personal pronouns refer to people: you, I, me, myself, who.

> *I rushed into the boat.*

Possessive pronouns indicate ownership: my, mine, yours, hers

> *I had to stay in my cabin all day.*

They can be used in questions:

> *Who would want to do that for a holiday?*

They can also be used to complete meaning in a sentence:

> *It's a good thing there was a shower on the boat so I could clean mud off myself.*

Distinguishing between the first-, second- and third-person pronouns

An account written in the first person uses pronouns such as 'I', 'me', 'myself', 'mine', 'we', 'us', 'ourselves' and 'our'.

An account written in the second person uses pronouns such as 'you' and 'your'.

A third person account uses pronouns such as 'he', 'she', 'it', 'his', 'hers', 'they' and 'theirs'.

Pronouns are used to mark gender: she, he, her, him and so on.

In using pronouns it is important for the children to make clear what the pronoun refers to. This should have been established in a previous sentence or earlier in the same sentence.

Punctuation pointers

Letter punctuation

Punctuation in the main body of the letter is the same as for any text. However, punctuation at the head of a letter varies according to how formal the letter is and whether one is following full punctuation rules or the more recent tendency to use the minimum of punctuation.

Some conventions vary over time. Recently the use of word processing has led to the removal of punctuation from the address headings in a letter. This is referred to as 'open punctuation'.

> *246 Stickleback Walk*
> *Smallstream*
> *SS98 7AZ*

According to the Plain English Campaign: 'Don't put commas after each line of the address, the greeting or the end line of the letter. You don't need full stops in initials of a person's name.'

It seems this type of punctuation has become optional.

> The children's version of these notes is on page 76 of the Resource book.

Writing features
Layout, structure and audience of informal letters

Informal private letters are personal documents not intended for publication and that have certain characteristics in common.

Layout

The writer's address goes at the top right-hand corner with the date underneath. It is not necessary to include the recipient's address.

'Dear…' goes on the next line against the left-hand margin. The main body of the letter is written below this.

An informal ending is used, such as 'Love from' for family or close friends and 'Best wishes' for other people. The signature will consist of the first name only because the reader knows the writer well.

Paragraphs should be used each time a new topic is introduced.

'P.S.' can be used for an afterthought.

It is important to emphasise the use of clear, neat, handwriting so the letter is legible and pleasant for the recipient to read.

Structure

There will be a tendency to be haphazard in writing ideas and thoughts as they come to mind but most informal letters usually recount events in chronological order. Some aspects might be written about in detail, including some colourful description.

> We climbed up a long, dark, winding, spiral stairway.

> We could see a long way, right to the distant horizon, but there was a sheer drop right in front of us!

Some amusing comments, jokes and anecdotes make the letter more lively and entertaining. For example, in Helen's letter, she tells how she accidentally jumped into deep mud when trying to moor the boat.

Informal letters often include questions that help to involve the reader in considering the content of the letter as well as providing something that the recipient can reply to. For example,

> 'Is your dad like that?'

Informal letters often contain quite routine and mundane, everyday aspects such as visits by relatives or doing various jobs around the house so any elements of surprise or excitement will add interest and enliven the content of the letter.

Writing for an audience

The matching of the writing to the audience is very important and aspects of style and structure should be explained to the children. They need to target the audience and direct their writing by choice of the subject matter, the tone of the letter and the type of language used.

An informal letter to a friend can include slang and words in common use by the age group. An older relative or friend may not understand or appreciate this type of language so it is better to use standard English.

Different subject matter may appeal to different age groups. The story of Helen's jump into the mud would appeal to all but, perhaps, the story involving the pike and the girl being pushed into the water might shock a grandmother who assumes Helen is always well behaved. The subject content may need to be modified according to the age of the reader and the relationship with the writer.

Notes and messages

It is not always necessary to write a complete letter. The most common form of message is now the email or text message. These are more like memos or telegrams than letters. While emails can be set out as a letter they usually are not.

In writing an email it is important to put the recipient's email address (return address is usually inserted automatically) and a subject in the subject line. There are few conventions. One rule is not to use all capital letters as this is taken to be rather discourteous 'shouting'. The email can begin with 'Hello', the Americanism 'Hi' or other greeting, such as 'Good morning' and tends to be more informal than conventional letter writing.

> There are helpful hints for children for writing informal letters on page 79 of the resource book.

Recounts
Formal letters

Email may seem to be taking over from letter writing today but there are still plenty of occasions where a formal letter is necessary. For example, the legal profession has been rather slow to accept electronic communication for all purposes and one is still frequently asked to 'confirm in writing' which usually entails a formal letter, with a signature, on paper. It is, therefore, still relevant and necessary for children to know how to write a carefully constructed and well-presented letter.

The importance of email is, however, acknowledged within this unit as there are some conventions to be observed with this type of communication when used for formal purposes.

A comparison between the informal letter in Unit 6 and the formal letters in this unit can provide an introduction to the difference in language used. In this unit the children will be introduced to the skills of writing for official purposes. There are a number of formal letter types. For example:

✦ To inform – for example, to give information about products, services, prices and availability.
✦ To protest – for example, about the treatment of animals or the closure of amenities.

✦ To complain – for example, about faulty goods or poor service.
✦ To persuade – for example, the local council to provide better services or people to donate money to charity.
✦ To give an opinion – for example, views on a television programme or a newspaper article.

Formal letters can often be used to recount an event and so are good examples to use when teaching the use of recount.

The children will learn the correct presentation, styles and tone according to the purposes of their letters. They will also consider the use of formal language to write letters that are precise and businesslike.

Recounts

Examples of formal letters

✦ Parents to schools requesting information, prospectus, brochure, etc.
✦ University to applicant offering a place on a course.
✦ Club secretary to a speaker asking for a speech to members.
✦ Charity to donor thanking for a donation.
✦ Organisation to competitor informing of a prize being won.
✦ Financial organisations providing information to customers.
✦ Tax office asking for details of income and expenses.

Websites

http://www.learn.co.uk/default.asp?WCI=Unit&WCU=4651

http://www.comedition.com/Business/properenglish.htm

The children's version of the letters is on page 86 of the resource book.

A letter to inform

246 Stickleback Walk
Smallstream
SS98 7AZ[1]

20th August 2003[2]

The Managing Director
Holiday Boats
River Terrace
Wroxham
NN98 00H[3]

Dear Sir or Madam[4]

I am[5] writing to say how very pleased we were with the boat we hired from you for our holiday on the Norfolk Broads, which commenced 3rd August 2003 for two weeks.[6]

We were particularly pleased with the attitude of your friendly and helpful staff. They were very keen to ensure we understood all aspects concerning the use of the boat.

The boat was in very good condition and very clean. All the equipment was in good working order and no faults developed despite the fact that our lively children made full use of all the facilities.[7] We had a most enjoyable holiday and definitely intend to return for more boating activities in the future.

Please pass on my comments to your staff and convey our thanks and appreciation to them.[8]

I hope this letter will encourage everyone concerned to keep up the high standards of service you so efficiently provide.[9]

Yours faithfully[10]

I Crawler[11]

I. Crawler[12]

A letter to request information

879 Patriot's Crescent
Hometown
Lancashire
HH5 9NW[1]

3rd February 2004[2]

The Manager
The Tourist Information Office
The Harbour
Kingsbridge
Devon
KK7 3SW[3]

Dear Sir or Madam[4]

We always prefer to take our holidays in England. I am writing to ask for information about your area of South Devon.[5]

I am[6] particularly interested in the cheaper bed and breakfast accommodation in your area. If possible, please send me addresses of farmhouses that have this type of accommodation.

[7]We have three children who enjoy spending time on the coast. It would, therefore, be particularly interesting to receive information about beaches within easy reach. I would also like to organise some pony trekking or horse riding for my family. Please supply details of any such opportunities.[8]

The ideal situation would be a farm near the coast, with accommodation and horse riding available. We will be particularly delighted if you are able to find us such an opportunity.[9]

General information about the South Hams area of Devon would be most welcome, plus details of other sources of information we may find in our local library.[10]

I look forward to receiving your reply.[11]

Yours faithfully[12]

[13]

Z. Mhetubou[14]

1. The writer's address in top right-hand corner. No commas or full stops are needed.

2. The date is written under writer's address.

3. The recipient's address is on the next line next to left margin.

4. The name or sex of the manager is not known so the titles 'Sir' or 'Madam' are used.

5. The opening sentences make the purpose of the letter very clear.

6. In formal letters the full forms of words 'I am' are used instead of the shortened 'I'm'.

7. Paragraphs in the main part of the letter give details of information required and why.

8. It is made clear what action is requested.

9. Further clarification builds on the previous paragraphs using formal language rather than 'It would be really good if you could find us a bed and breakfast farm near the coast with horse riding'.

10. The final paragraph sums up the main message of the letter.

11. A polite concluding comment indicating a reply is expected soon.

12. The writer does not know the name of the recipient so signs off with 'Yours faithfully'.

13. The writer's signature is included.

14. The writer's name is written legibly below the signature.

A letter to persuade

708 Manyhouses Terrace
Crampton
Wiltshire
SS9 6WW[1]

10th May 2003[2]

Mr G Funmaker
Parks and Gardens Department
The Council Offices
Circle Square
Boarham
Wiltshire
BB1 9WW[3]

Dear Mr Funmaker[4]

Improvements to the local playground[5]

The parents of Crampton greatly appreciate the fact that you have responded to previous requests for a playground for our children. I am now writing to ask you to consider the installation of more equipment in the playground.[6]

The playground has made a big difference to the opportunities for children to enjoy themselves in this overcrowded area of housing. It is good that they now have somewhere to play football without the dangers of doing so in the streets. However, some more equipment is needed because not every child wants to play football.[7]

The two swings are better than nothing but most playgrounds have a roundabout, a slide and climbing frames. On behalf of the parents and children of Crampton, I am asking you to investigate the possibility of obtaining such equipment to bring the playground up to the standard of most others.[8] It would also be much safer if a soft surface were to be installed.

I know the children would find these extra facilities very enjoyable and I hope these suggestions will be acted upon in the near future.[9]

I look forward to receiving a positive reply.[10]

Yours sincerely[11]

J Pushy[12]

J. Pushy
Chairman, Crampton Residents' Association.[13]

1	Own address in top right-hand corner.
2	The date written in full gives a good impression.
3	The recipient's address is on the next line next to left margin.
4	The recipient is addressed by name.
5	A clear heading is used in this letter, indicating the subject of the letter.
6	The opening paragraph very politely and clearly states the reason for writing.
7	The second paragraph develops the theme of the letter and becomes persuasive in tone.
8	Formal, businesslike vocabulary is used politely to clarify points.
9	This final paragraph reinforces the main request of the letter in a persuasive way and politely makes it clear a prompt reply would be welcome.
10	A polite concluding comment indicating a reply is expected. By including the word 'positive' the writer is hoping he has persuaded the recipient.
11	The recipient's name is used at the start of the letter so 'Yours sincerely' is used at the end.
12	The writer's signature is included.
13	The writer's name and status are written clearly below the signature.

Understanding the grammar and punctuation

Understanding the grammar and punctuation enables children to control the language they use and therefore to write effectively.

Grammar pointers

Help the children to be aware of the following when writing their letters.

Formal language

Formal language is used for letters to businesses and official organisations. The tone is impersonal. The reader feels distanced from the writer. The vocabulary has to be precise, accurate and correct. Typical phrases are worded in a conventional way:

> *I am writing to say...*

> *I look forward to receiving a positive reply.*

The tone is not friendly as in an informal letter to a friend or relative.

Slang is never used in formal letter writing.

Grammatical agreement of pronouns and verbs

A pronoun must agree with its noun in relation to person, gender and number plus the verb must agree with the pronoun.

The correct choice of verb is crucial as an error can be particularly irritating; for example, 'we *was* going out' instead of 'we *were* going out'. The verb has to be matched with the subject.

> **I am** *writing to say how very pleased* **we were** *with the boat.*

> **It is** *good that they now have somewhere to play football.*

The third person singular tense always ends in an 's'. I, you, we, they **run**. He **runs**.

As we do not use 'thou', the pronoun 'you' is followed by the plural form of the verb even when it refers to one person.

> **You are** *very clever.*

Punctuation pointers

Paragraphs

A paragraph is a group of sentences that cover one idea. The sentences in a paragraph are about the main idea of that paragraph.

It is often said that the reason for using paragraphs is to provide a pause or 'rest' for the reader. It provides an opportunity to stop and think about the content of several sentences about the same topic, before moving on.

A paragraph is variable in length. It may be only one sentence long or it may have several sentences.

One sentence in the paragraph is known as the topic sentence and contains the main idea for the whole paragraph. Quite often the topic sentence is the first sentence of the paragraph.

Examples of topic sentences

The main point is given:

> *The boat was in very good condition and very clean.*

An opinion or feeling is made clear:

> *We were particularly pleased with the attitude of your friendly and helpful staff.*

A reason, description or explanation may be made clear followed by more detail:

> *We have three children who enjoy spending time on the coast. It would, therefore, be particularly interesting to receive information about beaches within easy reach.*

The children's version of these notes is on page 89 of the resource book.

Writing features
Format, style and tone of formal letters

Letters written to someone for a specific purpose are usually written formally unless the person is a close friend or relative.

The purposes may be to:
+ give information;
+ ask for something;
+ praise or congratulate;
+ give an opinion;
+ complain about something or suggest improvements;
+ persuade someone.

The following needs to be explained to the children.

There is a substantial difference between writing a letter to a friend and writing a letter to someone in authority, such as their head teacher. A formal letter indicates respect and is appropriate when writing to most organisations, businesses and professional people. Polite expressions and correct grammar are used. No slang or over-familiar expressions are used.

Format

The children need to understand how to write, using the layout of a formal letter:
1. Own address in the top right-hand corner.
2. Date below own address.
3. Address of recipient on left-hand side of next line.
4. Dear (Sir, Madam or their name if known).
5. If writing to a woman and are uncertain about her title, use 'Dear Ms…'
6. If appropriate, a subject heading can come next.
7. Paragraphs to state the reason for writing, in a logical order, giving the details and politely making clear the action required.
8. Formal ending: 'Yours faithfully' is used if the recipient's name is not known and 'Yours sincerely' is used if the recipient's name is known.

Style

The style of this type of correspondence needs to be clear and crisp. The delivery should be as complete and accurate as possible. Relevance is important. Remind the children to keep it short and to the point.

Linking phrases should be used; for example, 'in addition' and 'what is more'. The last statement should round off the letter suitably.

I look forward to receiving your reply.

I know the children would find these extra facilities very enjoyable and I hope these suggestions will be acted upon in the near future.

Tone

The tone of a letter shows the writer's attitude towards the content of the letter. This can be explained to the children as similar to the tone of voice and language used in particular situations and when in particular moods. Angry and abusive comments in a letter of complaint could cause the reader to be offended and not secure appropriate cooperation in resolving the matter. It is important to state the case firmly but also to be polite and make reasonable requests and suggestions.

Use of emails in formal communications

Although there are still many situations where a formal signed letter is needed, particularly in connection with agreements and confirmation of legal matters, the email is now extensively used instead of the formal letter. These are more like memos or telegrams than letters.

Emails can be set out as formal letters. In fact, some traditional organisations even use their letter heading and logo in the body of the email so it looks exactly like a letter. More usually, however, the time-saving methods of email are used.

+ Only the recipient's email address has to be entered. The return address is usually inserted automatically.
+ Explain to the children that it is important to write a subject in the subject line. It is considered discourteous to omit this.
+ Do not use all capital letters as this is taken to be rather discourteous 'shouting'.
+ The email can begin with 'Dear …', 'Good Morning' or, to people who have already been contacted, 'Hello' or even the Americanism, 'Hi'.
+ Once contact has been established, correspondence is often rapidly exchanged and tends to become more informal than letter writing.
+ Because of increased problems with computer viruses, it is best to include everything in the email message box and not to send an attachment unless the recipient is expecting it.

Probably the most important aspect to explain to the children is that formal emails should be brief and very concise.

There are helpful hints for children for writing formal letters on page 92 of the resource book.

Recounts
Newspaper reports

Newspapers enjoy an enduring popularity despite all the other competing sources of news: television, Internet, radio and teletext. It seems the printed word is still the way the majority of people prefer to digest news and background information. It is easily available to read as and when the reader chooses to delve into the newspaper pages. Various types of newspapers report news in different ways and for varying sizes of readership. It is appropriate and interesting for the children to begin to investigate the range of different types, styles and layouts of the newspapers in preparation for regular use of this medium.

A local newspaper concentrates mainly on local news topics and covers them in detail. It usually covers a county, a large town or city or a group of villages. Many of the stories are about local people and how they have reacted to local and national events. Issues reported on include proposals for planned developments, crimes, sports and other events, traffic problems, changes to services and facilities, local council discussions and weather events such as snowfall and unusual rainfall causing flooding.

A national newspaper concentrates on news affecting the whole country but may also include some particularly interesting stories from local newspapers. International news figures prominently. In the main body of the newspaper there are articles and reports that tend to be more like the content of magazines. Depending on the type of newspaper, there may be substantial coverage of the activities of celebrities, royalty, glamorous events or an emphasis on political commentary and thought-provoking essays.

All newspapers have some similarities and tend to include headlines to attract attention, mainly short sentences, short paragraphs, columns, and various typefaces making text easy and quick to read. Photographs and quotations reinforce the truth or reality of the story.

For layout features of newspaper reports, refer to page 52.

Recounts

Examples of newspaper reports

Newspapers – plenty of local and national newspapers are available. Websites – most newspapers have websites with example pages and news items.

Greek Gazette by Paul Dowsell, Newspaper History series (Usborne,1997)

The Roman News by Philip Gates and Ghislaine Lawrence (Walker Books, 1994)

Websites

http://www.kidnews.com/news.html

http://news.bbc.co.uk/cbbcnews/default.stm

http://media.guardian.co.uk/

http://www.thenewspaper.org.uk/news/index.php3

Links to many National Newspapers' websites are on:

http://www.bl.uk/collections/national.html

The children's illustrated version of the newspaper reports is on page 99 of the resource book.

The Bleatbrook Chronicle[1]

LIFEBOAT GOAT RESCUE[2]

A herd of goats faced drowning when the River Chelwater burst its banks.[3]

GOATS TRAPPED BY FLOOD WATER[4]

The River Chelwater reached its highest ever level and suddenly broke through flood defences early on Saturday morning.[5] A small herd of goats were tethered in their shed at Buttfight Farm, near Bleatbrook. The water surged around their shed and trapped them.[6] As the water rose, they had to stand with front hooves high up on the shed wall to keep their heads above water. The rope tethers stopped them from escaping.

ANIMALS PANIC[7]

Loud panic-stricken bleating woke the farmer and his wife, Arthur (59) and Andrea Landworker (58). They rushed into the field and were immediately up to their waists in water. Unable to reach the goat shed, they could hear the awful sounds of their distressed animals trapped in the shed.

They hurried back to telephone for help. The local policeman reported an RNLI inshore lifeboat had come up river from the harbour and had rescued some people from flooded houses. An emergency radio call was made to the lifeboat crew.[8]

RNLI MAN USES AXE[9]

In the early light of dawn the lifeboat sped up the river to the flooded farm.

The water was[10] deep enough for the lifeboat to go straight to the goat shed. Lifeboatman Greg Bravemariner said afterwards, 'We could hear the bleating as the goats desperately tried to keep their heads above the rising water level but we could not open the shed door. I broke down the door with an axe. I tied a knife to a pole and used it to cut the tethers holding the goats down. They immediately swam past the boat but went the wrong way – towards the river!'[11]

SWIMMING GOATS ROUNDED UP BY LIFEBOAT

Lifeboat coxswain Andy Navigator explained, 'I had to steer the boat carefully round the swimming herd and turn them towards dry land. They quickly rushed up onto the next field – onto dry land. Mr. Landworker took the goats into a barn where a heater dried and warmed the shivering animals.'

Mr Landworker said, 'This came as a big shock. The river has not flooded for twenty years – not since the high bank was built to stop the floods. We are very pleased the lifeboat was nearby. This must be one of the most unusual rescues in the history of the lifeboat service! We will be moving the goat shed well away from the river flood plain.'[12]

---

1 This is a local newspaper with a story of what has happened on a farm in the local area.

2 Eye-catching headline in large bold letters. The wording rouses curiosity and interest.

3 Subheading gives brief details of the news item.

4 Further subheadings as single words or phrases indicate the contents of the paragraphs and break up the text in easy to read sections.

5 Topic sentence states the main cause of the event. The following sentences cover the details of what, where, when, who and how.

6 Dramatic words used: 'surge' and 'trapped'.

7 Another emotive subheading intended to attract the reader's attention to this section and to part of the page where there may be an advertisement beside the text.

8 Dramatic description of events, easy to read.

9 Headings and subheadings in the present tense.

10 The text is mainly in the past tense.

11 Quote from person involved gives interesting first-hand account.

12 In the closing paragraph there is a statement indicating what will happen to stop the same thing happening in the future.

The Hopscotch News[1]

HOUSES IN FLOODED AREAS MAY BE ABANDONED[2]

Flooding now far more frequent[3]
Angry homeowners demand more protection[4]

[5]The far more frequent flooding by the country's rivers has caused residents to demand more to be done to protect their homes from being swamped – sometimes several times a year. The alarming response from the Rivers Agency was that some often-flooded houses should be knocked down and the unfortunate residents rehoused away from the river.[6]

Home polluted by sewage

Mr. Duckfoot, 51, geography teacher, of Riverside Estate, Deepford, Yorkshire, said, 'The Earth's atmosphere is getting warmer. This causes more water to be evaporated, which, in turn, makes more rainfall. No one seems to understand the river is receiving more water from extra rainfall and it is running off into the river much more quickly from all the new buildings and roads. This causes the river to flood my home with smelly, muddy water polluted with sewage.'[7]

Flooding should be expected

The Rivers Agency has claimed everything possible has been done to stop flooding. Hundreds of millions of pounds have been spent building embankments and new drainage channels. Mr. Buckpass, 48, Rivers Agency spokesman insisted, 'If people choose to live on the flood plains beside rivers they should expect flooding to affect them.'[8]

He asked, 'Is it right for the majority of house owners to have to pay for more and more improvements and repairs through taxes and insurance premiums, to protect a small number of homes that should not have been built near rivers?' Buckpass went on to claim, 'House building companies should not build near rivers. If they do, they should pay for flood protection.'[9]

House builders may pay

The argument is about money for flood protection. Discussions are to take place next month, between the Rivers Agency and the house building companies, to move the families worst affected by flooding and to find the money to protect other houses more effectively.[10]

Understanding the grammar and punctuation

Understanding the grammar and punctuation enables children to control the language they use and therefore to write effectively.

Grammar pointers

Adjectives

Adjectives are **describing** words. In newspaper reports they are used for clarity *and* effect, for example, to arouse emotions and make a passage more dramatic.

> *Unable to reach the goat shed, they could hear the <u>awful</u> sounds of their distressed animals trapped in the shed.*

> *The <u>alarming</u> response from the Rivers Agency was that some often-flooded houses should be knocked down and the <u>unfortunate</u> residents rehoused away from the river.*

To help the children understand the importance of adjectives in newspaper reports, collect some samples of reports and delete the adjectives. Ask the children to comment on the effectiveness of the sentences without adjectives and then ask them to suggest appropriate ones. Their suggestions can be compared with the actual report. Another technique is to replace the adjectives used with other adjectives to see what this would do to the meaning of the sentence.

There can be confusion between adjectives and adverbs which modify verbs. It is worth pointing out that if the word is **ad**ded to a **verb** rather than a noun it is an **adverb** and not an adjective. Adverbs are also used to make descriptions more dramatic.

Verbs

Remind the children that a sentence must have a verb because it is concerned with the action taking place. Newspaper reports are full of accounts of activity and happenings.

The tense of a verb tells you when the action is taking place. There are three main tenses.

The past tense is used for what has happened.

The present tense is used for what is happening now.

The future tense is used for what is still to happen.

The past tense is used for most newspaper reports.

> *The River Chelwater <u>reached</u> its highest ever level and suddenly <u>broke</u> through flood defences early on Saturday morning.*

It may, however, be appropriate to use the future tense in some sentences to indicate what will or could happen next.

> *'We <u>will be moving</u> the goat shed well away from the river flood plain.'*

The **present** tense is often used in headlines and sub-headings.

> *Angry homeowners <u>demand</u> more protection.*

Punctuation pointers

Dialogue punctuation

Quotation marks (speech marks) are used in newspaper reports to show the actual words spoken by people who have witnessed events or expressed ideas, information and opinions. Double speech marks were the norm but single marks are now more common – probably because it is easier to select the single version on a keyboard. A comma, or sometimes a colon, is used before the quotation. Over-use of the word 'said' can be avoided by considering alternatives.

> *Lifeboat coxswain Andy Navigator <u>explained</u>, 'I had to steer the boat carefully round the swimming herd and turn them towards dry land.'*

Quotation marks are often used to enclose titles of books, newspapers, magazines, plays and so on.

The Hopscotch News is a fictitious title for a national newspaper.

> The children's version of these notes is on page 101 of the resource book.

Writing features
Layout and structure of newspaper reports

A comparison should be made between the writing features of newspaper reports in this unit and other types of reports in earlier units. Explain to the children that newspaper reports are written to inform the reader. Newspapers also want to appeal to readers in order to sell as many copies as possible. This leads to many of these publications adopting a style of writing and layout that is eye catching and often emotional, dramatic and quite sensational.

LIFEBOAT GOAT RESCUE
RNLI MAN USES AXE

Sometimes reporting may be biased in order to be provocative and stimulate discussion. Mostly, though, newspaper reports should leave the readers feeling they have been given various points of view and they understand exactly what has happened.

Layout

Headlines are intended to attract the reader's attention to a report. They are constructed in large bold print and include:
✦ short punchy sentences or phrases;
✦ the present tense;
✦ dramatic, sometimes exaggerated, statements;
✦ emphasis on the main point of the story;
✦ alliteration, puns, exclamations or slang.

Subheadings divide up the text into easy-to-read sections with an indication of the content. The subheading is often worded in a way that will arouse curiosity and encourage the reader to continue. This can be important to draw attention towards nearby advertisements, which provide the main income for the newspaper.

Columns are used for the layout. These make it easier for the reader to read quickly down the page without looking from side to side.

Captions next to photographs and illustrations link these with the text and draw the reader into the story. Side bars, inset text or boxes may contain related background information in easy-to-read separate sections.

The inverted pyramid

One method of writing newspaper articles is called 'the inverted pyramid'. This involves the most important or substantial items in an article being at the beginning. These include the five 'Ws' and one 'How':

✦ 'Who' names the subject of the story;
✦ 'What' tells the action that takes place;
✦ 'When' tells the time the action is happening;
✦ 'Why' explains the action;
✦ 'Where' describes the place where the action is happening;
✦ 'How' describes the manner of the action.

The second paragraph will add details to the story and subsequent paragraphs will provide the background information and other less important details.

This makes articles easy to read and easy to edit. The essentials of the story will still be included should the newspaper editor cut items from the end.

> There are helpful hints for children on writing a newspaper report on page 104 of the resource book.

Explanations
Encyclopaedias

An encyclopaedia can be a general reference book or it can be on a specific subject, such as sport or gardening. The differences between the encyclopaedia, the dictionary and other reference books should be explained to the children.

Using reference books that involve alphabetically ordered texts prepares children for making their own alphabetically ordered texts. A wide range of alphabetical directories can be used. As well as dictionaries and encyclopaedias the children should become familiar with the skill of using a telephone directory, an attendance register, a gazetteer at the end of an atlas and a book index.

The task of making alphabetically ordered texts will, in turn, improve their ability and speed in using reference sources.

This type of text involves the use of:
✦ an impersonal style;
✦ language to describe and differentiate;
✦ some technical language;
✦ the present tense for much of the text;
✦ linking words such as conjunctions.

Illustrations and diagrams are often used alongside encyclopaedia entries. Labelled or annotated diagrams add substantial clarification.

This unit provides the opportunity to practise many of the skills developed in the other units – particularly Units 1 to 5. Research skills are developed and the ability to summarise the content of a passage or text, plus the ability to identify the main points being made.

This type of writing can be linked with other curriculum areas, such as science, geography and history, thus extending its use outside the literacy hour.

Explanations

Examples of encyclopaedias

Children's Britannica Encyclopaedia Britannica

Hutchinson's Multimedia Encyclopaedia On CD-Rom

Encarta Microsoft CD-Rom

Compton's Home Library CD-Rom

The children's illustrated version of the encyclopaedia entries is on page 111 of the resource book.

Encyclopaedia extract

Chalk[1]

Chalk is a soft white rock.[2] It is a type of limestone that has formed on the bottom of the sea and is made up of millions of shells from tiny dead sea creatures. The main masses of chalk were formed between 140 and 70 million years ago. Some of this chalk has been pushed up by movements like those that cause earthquakes so that hills are made.[3] Chalk can be seen in the white cliffs at Dover where the hills have been worn away by the waves.[4]

Chalk was used[5] to write on blackboards in classrooms before felt pens and white boards replaced it. Chalk broken up into powder is used in making paper and paint and has been used in powder for cleaning teeth.

Glass

Glass is a hard transparent material which light easily passes through. It does not rot or dissolve so it lasts a long time. Window glass keeps out cold and rain but lets in light.[6] Bottles and windows[7] are often made of easily made cheaper glass, which is fragile and breaks easily. Some types of glass are made very strong by special processes such as adding layers of plastic between layers of glass. Water and other liquids cannot get through it therefore it is a good material for containers like bottles and jars. Glass mirrors reflect light. Glass can be shaped to make lenses that magnify and can be used in spectacles, telescopes and binoculars.

Glass is made out of pure white sand which is melted at a very high temperature. Other materials like powdered limestone are added to the sand to make different types of glass.[8] Glass is recycled by heating broken glass, melting it, then adding it to the melted sand. As it cools it is shaped to become solid glass window panes, drinking glasses, lenses, etc.

Granite

Granite is a very hard igneous rock. It is usually pink or grey and consists of quartz, feldspar and pieces of mica. Granite was formed ages ago when molten rock called magma slowly cooled below the Earth's surface.[9] Crystals of quartz which look like smoky glass, coloured feldspar crystals and shiny mica formed in the rock because the molten magma cooled slowly.

Because granite is very hard and strong, it is very good for making curbs, paving blocks and statues. It is also good for building large buildings although its hardness makes it difficult to cut granite to the right shape. This makes it expensive to use.[10]

Limestone

Most types of limestone are light grey in colour – almost white in some cases. Carboniferous limestone has cracks and joints in it that let water into the rock. The water often causes caves and potholes to form in this type of rock. Limestone is formed from sea shells and corals that have been pressed together on the sea floor. Layers of limestone have been pushed up by movements in the Earth's crust to form hills and mountains. This rock is easier to cut to the right sizes and shapes than granite so it is used in buildings. Limestone is dug up in quarries and is used in making cement. Crushed limestone is used for the surface of roads and is put into furnaces with coal and iron ore when making steel.

---

1 Clear heading. Entries are arranged in alphabetical order.

2 Simple statement describing the item. Use of present tense.

3 More detail expanding the description and explaining formation.

4 An example to illustrate the explanation.

5 Use of the item explained.

6 Description and details of properties. Includes use of technical language, such as 'transparent'.

7 Use of product.

8 Information on process of making a type of glass.

9 Formation of the item is explained.

10 Properties of the rock are linked with uses by using the conjunction 'because'.

Rock

The Earth's crust is made of rock. Rocks are mostly solid, hard and heavy. Some are harder than others. Granite is very hard but chalk is soft. Slate breaks up into waterproof sheets of hard but quite brittle rock. Rocks are made up of minerals, rather like making a cake. The amounts of mineral ingredients are different for different types of rock. Some rocks have actually been baked by volcanic heat, making them hard like a burnt cake.[11] A rock can be made from the remains of living things. Coal is a rock made from dead plants pressed very hard together. Limestone is made from huge numbers of seashells pressed together. Iron ore is a rock which can be heated to a very high temperature so that liquid iron comes out and can be used to make steel.

Slate

Slate is a hard but quite brittle rock. It is a grey rock which is usually seen as flat sheets used on the roof of a building to keep out the cold and rain.[12] It is a rock made of very tiny pieces of other rocks that have been worn away into powder. This powdered rock, called clay, has then been pressed together underground.[13] It splits easily into flat, thin, smooth sheets that are waterproof. As well as being used for roof tiles, slate has, in the past been used as a sheet to write on with chalk. Each child in a classroom would have had a slate and a piece of chalk to write on the slate. This was much cheaper than using paper.[14]

Steel

Steel is a silvery, light grey metal - a very hard and very strong material -that is made by humans from rocks.[15] The rocks used are iron ore, limestone and coal. These are put into a furnace and heated to a very high temperature so that the rocks melt and join together. When the liquid cools it becomes steel. Steel is used to make a huge number of different things in factories. Some examples are car bodies, knives and forks, the framework of buildings, furniture and washing machines.[16]

11 Description with a comparison to aid understanding.

12 Description and use linked together.

13 This statement, using commas, clarifies the meaning of clay.

14 Historical note on past use.

15 Use of dashes to separate and emphasise a statement.

16 Examples used to clarify explanation. A labelled picture or diagram with a caption could also be included for further clarification.

Understanding the grammar and punctuation

Understanding the grammar and punctuation enables children to control the language they use and therefore to write effectively.

Grammar pointers

Joining sentences using conjunctions

A conjunction is a word that links clauses or sentences.

Children tend to write in short sentences. The use of conjunctions makes it possible to construct complex sentences, thereby also introducing more variety to the writing.

> *It is a type of limestone **that** has formed on the bottom of the sea **and** is made up of millions of shells from dead tiny sea creatures.*

As well as using the obvious 'and' there are many other conjunctions that can be used instead of this often over-used word.

Examples of conjunctions include: after, although, as, because, before, if, since, so, that, though, until, unless, when, whenever, where, wherever, whereas, while.

> *Granite is good for building large buildings **although** its hardness makes it difficult to cut to the right shape.*

A sentence can be made more effective and stronger by the careful choice of a conjunction to link clauses. More meaning can be conveyed by using the right conjunction. Consider how much more effective is the use of **because** rather than **and** in this sentence:

> *Wood is easier to make into things than rock or steel **because** it can be cut and shaped more easily.*

Punctuation pointers

Commas and dashes

Commas are often used to mark grammatical boundaries. They are used after a subordinate clause which begins a sentence.

> *Because granite is very hard and strong, it is very good for making curbs, paving blocks and statues.*

Dashes can be used to indicate a break between subordinate and main clauses and to emphasise a word or phrase.

> *Steel is a silvery, light grey metal – a very hard and very strong material that is made by humans from rocks.*

Simple sentences should not be linked together with a comma. They should be joined by a conjunction (or in some cases, by a semi-colon).

The children's version of these notes is on page 113 of the Resource book.

Writing features
Writing an encyclopaedia entry

Planning

Explain to the children how to research the necessary information using a variety of sources. This will revise note taking introduced in Unit 5. Reference books on particular topics, for example, building materials, can be used as well as children's encyclopaedias in book, Internet and CD-Rom format. The children should, as far as possible, summarise the main points and write the information in their own words.

The information should then be organised and the writing of the entry planned. Most encyclopaedia entries will include, as appropriate, a description of the item's appearance, details of its location, structure, properties, formation, growth, manufacture and use. The intention is to make sure it is easy and quick to read, in a logical order and is easy to understand.

A bold title should be used to make it clear what the information is about.

A formal and impersonal style of writing should be used. The use of examples and comparisons can be used to any clarify points made. It is important to emphasise the information should be for someone who does not know much about the topic. This is why they are consulting the encyclopaedia.

Devices for presenting text

The use of titles in the large, dark print or capital letters and subheadings in bold but less prominent print should be explained. Capital letters, enlarged or italicised print and headings can be used.

Alphabetical order

The use of alphabetical order should be revised along with practice in using dictionaries, directories and encyclopaedias. Once the children have understood the method involved they should be ready to apply the principles to make their own alphabetically ordered texts.

Illustrations

Photographs, sketches and diagrams are an important part of explanations. A diagram must have a clear title and labels. These draw attention to the specific parts of the illustration and clarify the accompanying explanation.

As well as drawing their own illustrations, children can cut them out of newspapers, leaflets and magazines.

> There are helpful hints for children for writing an encyclopaedia entry on page 116 of the Resource book.